Be Still and Know

Be Still and Know

Know

A Study in the Life of Prayer

Michael Ramsey

COWLEY PUBLICATIONS
Cambridge ✦ Boston
Massachusetts

Be Still and Know was first published by Fount Paperbacks, London, in 1982, and Seabury Press, New York, in 1983.

Published in the United States of America by Cowley Publications, a division of the Society of St. John the Evangelist. No portion of this book may be reproduced, stored in or introduced into a retrieval system, or transmitted, in any form or by any means—including photocopying—without the prior written permission of Cowley Publications, except in the case of brief quotations embodied in critical articles and reviews.

Except where otherwise noted, all biblical quotations are from the *Revised Standard Version of the Bible,* copyrighted 1946, 1952 and © 1971, 1973 by the Division of Christian Education of the National Council of the Churches of Christ in the U.S.A..

Library of Congress Cataloging-in-Publication Data
Ramsey, Michael, 1904-1988.
  Be still and know.
  1. Prayer—Biblical teaching. 2. Bible. N.T.—Criticism, interpretation, etc. 3. Prayer. I. Title.
BV228.R35 1983
248.3   83-4765
                                                                                    CIP
ISBN 1-56101-083-9

This book is printed on acid-free recycled paper and was produced in the United States of America.

Second Printing

Cowley Publications
28 Temple Place
Boston, Massachusetts 02111

Contents

Preface

This book has a single theme, but its two parts are different in form. The first part is a study of the Prayer of Jesus and the understanding of prayer in St. Paul, St. John and the Letter to the Hebrews as well as in the story of the Transfiguration. The second part is more directly pastoral in form, and deals with some of the practical aspects of Christian praying, with a digression on some lessons from the English Mystics of the fourteenth century and the Spanish Mystics of the sixteenth, in the belief that they speak to our contemporary world.

The title *Be Still and Know* describes a recurring plea in the book that stillness and silence are of supreme importance and that the neglect of them is damaging to the Christian life. There are signs however of a recovery of the contemplative spirit with the realization that contemplation is an exposure to the divine love powerful in its effects upon a human life.

Michael Ramsey

Prologue

There are many people who warm to the Christian faith and yet find the idea of prayer perplexing or even intellectually suspect. It is sometimes asked: amidst the vast range of desperate human need can we believe that a God of love and compassion gives selective favors to certain people because some other people may have prayed for them? Others ask: are we sure that the praying which goes on in churches and elsewhere really affects the course of events in the world around us?

We need, however, to see Christian prayer not as an isolated religious exercise but as an aspect of a manysided converse between human beings and their Creator. In the Christian belief God makes himself known to mankind in many ways: through the beauty of nature, through the stirrings of conscience, through inspired men and women and writings, through events of history, and supremely through Jesus Christ. To these "utterances" of God the human response is no less multiple: by gratitude and trust and love, by awe and wonder, by grief and contrition, by acts of practical service and the pursuit of a way of life. In this response there is movement of the heart and mind and will towards God, partly but not always wholly expressed in words. The entire God-man relationship is often described by the biblical writers, Jewish and Christian, in the images of speaking and hearing. But verbal conversation, as when a voice says "Samuel, Samuel" and a response comes "Here I am," is but a small fraction in a relationship containing word and silence, passivity and action. Such is the context of prayer in Christianity.

It seems to follow that, in understanding the true nature of prayer, it is a mistake to draw too rigidly the frontier between prayer and life. The separation of them, which has sadly recurred in history, can lead to caricatures of both. Thus prayer can become a pious or aesthetic or cultural pursuit, whose goal seems less than the God who loves mankind; and the Christian life can become a kind of aggressive busyness which misses the humility and the inner peace which communion with God can bring.

If the interweaving of prayer and life within the converse with God is realized then the two questions mentioned at the beginning of this prologue may appear less daunting.

(1) Does petitionary prayer imply an arbitrary selectivity in God's graciousness? It need not do so. If God is a God of love and compassion who uses the cooperation of human wills to fulfill his purpose, the petitionary prayer of a Christian will be both an offering of himself and a caring request on behalf of others, both a "Lord, make me an instrument of your peace" and a "Lord, use my caring to bless X and Y and Z." When he thus puts his caring at God's disposal he will be confident that good will come to X and Y and Z, but he will not suppose that God's graciousness will halt with them. The teaching of Jesus suggests that God wants us to bring our specific desires to him, and to try to relate them to his purpose. We need not think that God will limit his use of our caring to those whom we name because we care.

(2) Is it credible that the praying which goes on in churches and elsewhere makes a difference to the world, apart perhaps from to those who do the praying? If prayer

and life are interwoven in the way described then the right question may be not: "What good does prayer do?" but "What good does the praying Christian do?" The praying Christian is one whose prayer is part of a converse with God which includes actions and orientations as well as words. Through the centuries, despite the failures and the scandals, the impact of Christianity in creating not a few Christlike lives has been through Christians for whom prayer has been an integral part of their sharing in the divine love. The promises of Jesus about the results of prayer are corroborated by recurring empirical evidence.

At the present time there has been in the West a trend of feeling towards the contemplative aspect of prayer, and many have looked to Eastern religions for contemplative practice, partly as a result of the Church's sad neglect of its own contemplative tradition. It is not, however, always realized either by seekers of contemplation or by its critics that contemplation is not only a quest of the inner peace of God but an exposure to the love of God with intercessory outreach. We learn from a contemplative such as Thomas Merton that the movement of the soul away from the world into the life of God is a movement also into the world's heart. The renewal of contemplation in the Church may help to renew caring service towards the world.

Concerning intercession: the Church is called to be a community which speaks to the world in God's name and speaks to God from the middle of the world's darkness and frustration. The prayer with beautiful buildings and lovely music must be a prayer which also speaks from the places where men and women work, or lack work, and are sad and hungry, suffer and die. To be near to the love of God is to be near, as Jesus showed, to the darkness of the world. That is the "place of prayer."

The first part of this book is about the prayer of Jesus. For Christians Jesus is the teacher of prayer, and the one whose own prayer is the source of our prayer and the power for its renewal. His prayer is a converse with the Father which includes the obedience of his life and death, and while it belongs to another world it is set in the darkness of the world we know.

Part One

Chapter 1

The Prayer of Jesus

T he prayer of Christian people draws its inspiration from the prayer of Jesus. By the action of the Holy Spirit they make the prayer of Jesus their own, as the vivid words of St. Paul tell us:

> For you did not receive the spirit of slavery to fall back into fear, but you have received the spirit of sonship. When we cry, "Abba! Father!" it is the Spirit himself bearing witness with our spirit that we are children of God, and if children, then heirs, heirs of God and fellow heirs with Christ, provided we suffer with him in order that we may be glorified with him. (Romans 8:15-17)

Here indeed is a new intimacy of prayer derived from Jesus' own prayer.

It has been held, notably by the scholar Joachim Jeremias, that the use of the little child's form of address, *Abba,* in prayer by Jesus was entirely unique. Other scholars however have queried this, pointing to evidence of the use of the word by charismatic Jews of the time. What is certain however is that the regular prayers of Jews in home and synagogue did not speak to God with such intimacy. God was the King and Father of the nation rather than the intimate father of each and every person. Quite apart from the word *Abba* something new and creative was happening when Jesus not only prayed to God simply as "Father" but also described God in his teaching as "the Father" or "my Father" and spoke to the disciples of "your Father." That Jesus spoke of "my Father," and of "your Father" in relation to the disciples, suggests that his own sonship is very distinctive and that their sonship is by adoption and derivation.

So we study first the prayer of Jesus and then the prayer of the early Christians. How he taught the disciples to pray is important for all time, and it may prefigure how he teaches us. How he prayed himself may be more significant still, in that our prayer is created and sustained by his.

It is not the purpose of the evangelists to describe the inner life of Jesus in the manner of a religious biography. Rather do the traditions in the gospels tell of the mission of Jesus to proclaim the Kingdom of God by his teaching and mighty works and to suffer and to die. But many incidents show that the mission is in the context of a relation between Jesus and the Father, and within this relation prayer has its powerful place. While incidents of prayer occur in each of the first three gospels (known as the synoptic gospels) it is St. Luke who emphasizes the prayer of Jesus, telling of his praying at some of the crucial happenings in his ministry. Each of the synoptic writers records the prayer of Jesus in agony in the Garden of Gethsemane.

The little which Mark tells about prayer within the ministry of Jesus is very significant. He records two episodes which together suggest that prayer is the source of power whereby the work of Jesus in teaching and healing is fulfilled. The first episode is near the beginning of the account of the Galilean ministry.

> In the morning, a great while before day, he rose and went out to a lonely place, and there he prayed. And Simon and those who were with him followed him, and they found him and said to him, "Every one is searching for you." And he said to them, "Let us go on to the next towns, that I may preach there also; for that is why I came out." (Mark 1:35-37)

It seems right to infer that the prayer of Jesus, a great while before day, was an intimate part of the work of that day. This is indeed suggested by the other episode. When Jesus returns to the disciples after the Transfiguration on the Mount described in Mark 9, he finds them helplessly trying to heal a boy suffering from demonic possession. The disciples' efforts have been in vain and Jesus says to them,

> This kind cannot be driven out by anything but prayer. (Mark 9:29)

The two passages suggest that for Jesus as for the disciples prayer is of the essence of the work of God.

Here are the occasions when Luke mentions that Jesus was praying at critical moments in his ministry, before we come to the Passion:

> Now when all the people were baptized, and when Jesus also had been baptized and was praying, the heaven was opened, and the Holy Spirit descended upon him in bodily form, as a dove, and a voice came from heaven, "Thou art my beloved son; with thee I am well pleased." (Luke 3:21-22)

In these days he went out into the hills to pray; and all night he continued in prayer to God. And when it was day, he called his disciples, and chose from them twelve, whom he named apostles. (Luke 6:12-13)

Now about eight days after these sayings he took with him Peter and John and James, and went up on the mountain to pray. And as he was praying, the appearance of his countenance was altered, and his raiment became dazzling white. (Luke 9:28-29)

He was praying in a certain place, and when he ceased, one of his disciples said to him, "Lord, teach us to pray, as John taught his disciples." (Luke 11:1)

On most of these occasions we are told nothing of the content of the prayer of Jesus, but we can be sure that the prayer linked the particular event with the continuing communion of Jesus with the Father. It is in intimacy with the Father that his mission is carried out from the divine affirmation of his sonship at his baptism right through to his own affirmation of it when he commits himself to the Father in the hour of death. Nor can we doubt that there was at the center of his own prayer the theme of the Kingdom, the Name, and the Will which he taught the disciples in the Lord's Prayer.

Now for the occasions when the gospels record the words used by Jesus in prayer. There is first the episode sometimes known as the Great Thanksgiving, and it is told in the common tradition used in Matthew and in Luke. In Matthew chapter eleven it comes at the climax of words of teaching about the role of Jesus in relation to the Baptist. In Luke chapter ten it comes after the return of the Seventy from their mission, and Jesus is described as rejoicing in the Spirit as he makes the utterance of praise. Matthew's text runs:

> I thank thee, Father, Lord of heaven and earth, that thou hast hidden these things from the wise and understanding and revealed them to babes; yea, Father, for such was thy gracious will. (Matthew 11:25-26; cf. Luke 10:21)

There follow words about the relation of the Father and the Son:

> All things have been told to me by my Father; and no one knows the Son except the Father, and no one knows the Father except the Son and any one to whom the Son chooses to reveal him. (Matthew 11:27; cf. Luke 10:22)

These words are not part of the prayer so much as an affirmation of that union of the Son with the Father which underlies all the prayers of Jesus. The words affirm a high doctrine of sonship. Some scholars have held that for this reason the words represent a late development in the tradition, perhaps in a Hellenistic setting. Others however think that the language is thoroughly Semitic and that the meaning is, "As only a father knows his son so also only a son knows his father and he to whom the son wants to reveal it." In this case the words are less a doctrinal affirmation than an analogy of a father-son relation. On either understanding a deep intimacy is described. It is in that intimacy that Jesus fulfills his mission.

At the supper Jesus tells Simon that he has been praying to the Father that the faith of the disciples may not fail.

Simon, Simon, behold, Satan demanded to have you, that he might sift you like wheat, but I have prayed for you that your faith may not fail; and when you have turned again, strengthen your brethren. (Luke 22:31)

The faith of the disciples did in the event fail and it was restored in a new depth. It may therefore be that the Father's response to the request of Jesus was to allow the loyalty of disciples to fail in the certainty that through their failure they will be freed from self-reliance and brought to a faith that is a true death to self.

After the supper there comes the scene in the Garden of Gethsemane, with the agony of Jesus and his prayer that the cup may pass from him and that the Father's will shall be done. Near to Jesus are three chosen disciples whom he desires to be with him, but they sleep despite his command to them to watch and to pray. The episode comes in each of the synoptics. Here is Mark's version.

And they went to a place which was called Gethsemane; and he said to his disciples, "Sit here, while I pray." And he took with him Peter and James and John, and began to be greatly distressed and troubled. And he said to them "My soul is very sorrowful, even to death; remain here, and watch." And going a little farther, he fell on the ground and prayed that, if it were possible, the hour might pass from him. And he said, "Abba, Father, all things are possible to thee; remove this cup from me; yet not what I will, but what thou wilt." And he came and found them sleeping, and he said to Peter, "Simon, are you asleep? Could you not watch one hour? Watch and pray that you may not enter into temptation; the spirit indeed is willing, but the flesh is weak." And again he came and found them sleeping, for their eyes were very heavy; and they did not know what to answer him. And he came the third time, and said to them, "Are you still sleeping and taking your rest? It is enough; the hour has come; the Son of man is betrayed into the hands of sinners. Rise, let us be going; see, my betrayer is at hand." (Mark 14:32-42)

Here, instead of the unswerving obedience of Jesus to the Father, there is, in the words of the New English Bible, "horror and dismay," and an agonizing blending of shrinking and acceptance. How did the prayer used by Jesus come to be known and recorded when the only witnesses were asleep? Perhaps it had been known to them that in Jesus there had been the shrinking of body and nerve from the ordeal, and this knowledge may have been put into the words of a prayer in part from Old Testament language and in part from the "thy will be done" of the "Our Father." But a tradition that Jesus underwent an agony of this kind is found also in Hebrews 5:17, and in John 12:27. Jesus is depicted as one with us in our frailty, not indeed of moral weakness but of body and nerve, and one with the Father in the power to turn every faculty towards the Father's purpose. Amidst his own agony, Jesus is still the pastor caring for the disciples and as their pastor he walks over to them and speaks to them, eager that they may be watching and praying to be saved from their own trial when it comes to them, as immediately it does. The theme of watching and praying recurs in the early Church sometimes in connection with the crisis of the Lord's coming.

Here is the passage in the letter to the Hebrews which strikingly recalls the agony of Jesus.

> In the days of his flesh, Jesus offered up prayers and supplications, with loud cries and tears, to him who was able to save him from death, and he was heard for his godly fear. Although he was a Son, he learned obedience through what he suffered; and being made perfect he became the source of eternal salvation to all who obey him, being designated by God a high priest after the order of Melchizedek. (Hebrews 5:7-10)

Two misunderstandings of this passage should be avoided. "He learned obedience" does not mean he learned to obey, for Hebrews makes it clear that Jesus was obedient from his coming into the world. Rather did he learn the full meaning of what obedience involved. "Being made perfect" does not mean "becoming morally perfect." "To perfect" has in Hebrews the special meaning of "to fit for a particular role," in this case the role of his heavenly priesthood.

We pass from the Garden of Gethsemane to the Hill of Calvary. Here Mark, followed by Matthew, records the prayer of the desolation of Jesus.

> And when the sixth hour had come, there was darkness over the whole land until the ninth hour. And at the ninth hour Jesus cried with a loud voice, "Eloi, Eloi, lama sabachthani?" which means, "My God, my God, why hast thou forsaken me?" (Mark 15:33-34)

Mark is depicting the death of Jesus as happening in physical darkness and spiritual loneliness. All the disciples seem to have deserted him, both the men crucified with him revile him, the leaders of the people are jeering, he is utterly alone, and now in the loneliness he cries out asking why God has deserted him.

Jesus is reciting the opening words of Psalm 22, a psalm which begins with words of desolation and passes on to words of triumph. Some think that Jesus would be reciting the whole psalm and that therefore he would be speaking and thinking of triumph no less than of desolation. But as Mark seems to be presenting the scene in terms of unrelieved darkness and loneliness, it may be that the cry tells of desolation only, Jesus entering into the depths of a world alienated from God and his presence. But if Jesus is thus in the depths, it is divine love which has brought him there. And what Mark depicts as desolation, John will depict as glory.

Mark and Matthew tell only of the prayer of desolation. Luke, whose account lessens the sense of loneliness by telling of the compassion of Jesus reaching out to those around him, records other prayers of Jesus on Calvary. Jesus prays for the soldiers who crucify him, commending them to the Father's compassion. "Father, forgive them; for they know not what they do" (Luke 23:34). Their ignorance is to be pitied. It is not only an ignorance of the divine Sonship of Jesus, it is an ignorance of his and their common humanity; not recognizing humanity they are treating man like a thing. To the depth of this blind and dark ignorance may the divine compassion reach. Finally, omitting the cry of desolation, Luke tells of Jesus committing himself to the Father in death: "Father, into thy hands I commend my spirit." Obedience to the Father, thanksgiving to the Father, intimacy with the Father have marked the mission of Jesus from first to last.

If the prayer of desolation recorded by Mark tells of the lonely and unshareable aspect of the Passion, Luke tells of that aspect which is to be shared in the lives of Christian disciples. Thus Stephen the first martyr is described by

Luke in the Acts as praying for his murderers, "Lord lay not this sin against them," and, like Jesus, commending himself to the Father. Following the example of the Son of Man in death he has, as he dies, a glimpse of the Son of Man in glory (Acts 7:55-60).

Such is the prayer of Jesus in his life on earth as the traditions in the first three gospels describe it. His prayer is the prayer of one who is deeply one with the Father while he shares in the frustrations of humanity. We have yet to see how John interprets the prayer of Jesus in terms of the giving of glory to the Father, a glory which is at once both heavenly and revealed in suffering and death.

Chapter 2

Teaching the Disciples

W hat did Jesus teach the disciples about prayer, and how did he teach it? The first three gospels tell us much, and the fourth gospel seems to draw together the themes and their interpretation.

There are two accounts of the giving of the Lord's Prayer by Jesus to the disciples. In Matthew the occasion is the Sermon on the Mount. Jesus has been deploring the long-winded and verbose prayers of some who think that the repetition of many words will impress God. And he gives his hearers a pattern prayer which has few words but great themes. In Luke the occasion is that Jesus has been praying alone, and when he finishes the disciples ask him to teach them to pray. We can picture to ourselves the occasions.

In the two accounts the wording of the prayer is different. Here is the text as the Revised Standard Version gives it.

Our Father who art in heaven	Father,
Hallowed be thy name.	Hallowed be thy name.
Thy kingdom come,	Thy kingdom come.

Thy will be done,	
On earth as it is in heaven.	
Give us this day our	Give us each day our
daily bread;	daily bread;
And forgive us our debts	And forgive us our sins,
As we also have	For we ourselves
forgiven our debtors;	forgive every one
	who is indebted to us;
And lead us not into	And lead us not into
temptation,	temptation.
But deliver us from evil.	(Luke 11:2-4)
(Matthew 6:9-13)	

We notice first that in neither of these texts does the RSV include the familiar doxology "For thine is the kingdom, the power and the glory, for ever and ever." These words are omitted in some of the most important of the Greek manuscripts, and it is fairly certain that they are not part of the original prayer, being added in the use of the Church at an early date. It was customary for Jews to end their prayers with a thanksgiving, and only likely that the early Christians would do the same; indeed the themes of the Lord's Prayer themselves seem to burst with thanksgiving.

The differences between the texts of Matthew and Luke are at once noticeable. How are they to be explained? Luke's account is short and Matthew's is longer, with some phrases of a Jewish liturgical kind. Perhaps the two versions represent the forms of the prayer used respectively in a Jewish Christian and a Gentile Christian community. Perhaps Matthew's text is original and Luke has abbreviated it for Gentile Christian use. More probably Luke's text is original and Matthew has enlarged it with a little language of Jewish paraphrase. The single word of address, Father, in Luke corresponds, as we have seen, to a mode of address used by Jesus.

Is it however disappointing for us that we cannot be sure of the exact words of the prayer? Not if we realize that while the hearers of Jesus would have cherished the exact words, the value for ourselves is not in a set of words so much as a set of themes. "Pray like this" says Jesus in Matthew's account; and this we can do with heart and mind and imagination focused upon the Father, the Kingdom, the Will, the Daily Bread, the Forgiveness of Sins, and the Deliverance from Evil. Thus, the bodily and spiritual needs of ourselves and of mankind are lifted into the orbit of God's purpose with the conviction that the Kingdom and the glory are his. "Pray like this."

Father. The theme is shown a little differently in the two versions. In Luke the single word of address "Father" recalls Jesus' own intimacy with the Father, an intimacy from which the disciples are learning. In Matthew "Our Father" tells of the community of disciples who will be praying. The words "in heaven" renew the Jewish sense of God's transcendence. Thus both versions of the prayer begin in a meditative way. Those who pray will let heart and mind and imagination dwell upon God's supremacy, compassion and care for his own. We are listening to God's word to us before we bring our requests to him.

Hallowed be thy name. Let the lives of those who pray, and the lives of all mankind and the created world, do honor to the name of the Father who created them all. Let the Father hallow his own name through the disciples' response.

Kingdom. The disciples dwell upon God's eternal sovereignty and ask that the sovereignty may be realized in the world. It is meanwhile the mission of Jesus to proclaim

God's sovereignty, and his mighty works and his teaching testify to its nearness or perhaps its actual presence. The disciples' personal desires and longings are still with them, and Jesus encourages them in many parts of his teaching to speak to the Father about these. But both the priority of the Kingdom and the petition "thy will be done" bid them be learning to test their desires and needs within the orbit of the Father and the Kingdom.

Our daily bread. The Greek word translated "daily" probably means "for tomorrow"; and it is thought by some scholars that behind the Greek is an Aramaic phrase meaning "for today and tomorrow." So the disciples ask that God's good providence will so order things that we shall not be in want and shall be free from worry about the coming day. But it is in the context of God's Kingdom and its righteousness that we pray; and the word "our" will tell of our fellow human beings near and far, and it will be a prayer in unselfishness, brotherhood and compassion.

It is suggested by Jeremias and others that the morrow and the bread in the prayer refer to the age to come and the heavenly food which is the Bread of Life. Jeremias, who urges this eschatological interpretation of the prayer, adds however that it need not exclude reference to immediate daily needs. The prayer will be that the new age and its heavenly food may here and now be present helping us in the tasks of today and tomorrow.

Forgive us. We ask God to forgive us, knowing that he will do so only if we ourselves are forgiving. If we are unforgiving we may not expect God's forgiveness. What if our unforgivingness is what most needs God's forgiveness? To acknowledge this may be the first step in our repentance.

One further theme comes in Matthew's version of the prayer. It is the theme of tribulation and evil, **lead us not**

into temptation and deliver us from evil. Temptation is man's inevitable experience and it is the experience of Jesus in his life on earth. If the Greek word here is rightly taken as temptation the meaning may be, as some of the ancient Fathers suggested, "do not bring us into such temptation as we shall be unable to bear." But perhaps the Greek word means rather "tribulation," the catastrophic trial which would precede the coming of the Messianic age. The disciples will pray to be delivered from that. Protection from the evil one is urgently to be prayed for. Both temptation and tribulation may by God's grace be endurable in the growth of holiness and in the doing of God's will, but not if the evil one snatches them for his own evil purposes. It is from that that we pray to be saved.

If these words of the prayer are indeed related to the trials preceding the Messianic age, does this make them remote from our own needs and our own day? Not so, if we remember that every coming of the power of God into the world happens through pain and cost, and every growth in our own holiness and Christlikeness happens also through pain and cost. The grace of God can turn the pain and cost to wonderful account, and we pray that the evil one may not use them for his evil ends.

Pray in this way. So the "Our Father" takes the needs and the agonizing conflicts of mankind and lifts them into the realm of the Kingdom and the Father. So close is the prayer to Jesus himself that we may fairly say that Christian prayer means not only the Lord's Prayer but the Lord's Prayer and the Lord.

From the Lord's Prayer we turn to other teaching concerning prayer which Jesus gave to the disciples according to the synoptic tradition.

In the Sermon on the Mount the giving of the Lord's Prayer is preceded by two severe criticisms of some contemporary practices (Matthew 6:5-8). One criticism, which we have already noticed, is of those who indulge in long-winded phrases in their prayers. The other criticism is of those who pray ostentatiously in public, to be observed and admired, and Jesus in contrast urges that prayer should be in the privacy of a person's own house. Later in the Sermon there is teaching about perseverance and confidence in prayer, "ask and ye shall receive, seek and ye shall find," teaching which Luke has in another context (Matthew 7:7-12; Luke 11:9-13).

Elsewhere in the synoptic gospels the most prominent theme of teaching about prayer is the need for perseverance, faith, and unrelenting expectation. One instance of this teaching comes in Mark. It is after the incident of the cursing of the fig tree, when the disciples are astonished at what has happened and Jesus says to them:

> Have faith in God. Truly, I say to you, whoever says to this mountain, "Be taken up and cast into the sea," and does not doubt in his heart, but believes that what he says will come to pass, it will be done for him. Therefore I tell you, whatever you ask in prayer, believe that you receive it, and it will be yours. And whenever you stand praying, forgive, if you have anything against any one; so that your Father also who is in heaven may forgive you your trespasses. (Mark 11:22-26)

Here too the call for faith and perseverance in prayer is linked with the insistence upon a forgiving spirit.

It is however in Luke's gospel that more teaching about persistence in prayer is given. In chapter eleven the episode of Jesus praying is, as we have seen, followed by the request for teaching about prayer and the giving of the Lord's Prayer in its Lucan form. Then follows a parable about persistence in prayer and sayings on the theme, sayings which Matthew includes in the Sermon on the Mount. The parable is that of the Friend at Midnight, with the theme that persistent asking lends to the granting of even a tiresome request. Then come the sayings:

> And I tell you, Ask, and it will be given you; seek, and you will find; knock, and it will be opened to you. For every one who asks receives, and he who seeks finds, and to him who knocks it will be opened. What father among you, if his son asks for a fish, will instead of a fish give him a serpent; or if he asks for an egg, will give him a scorpion? If you then, who are evil, know how to give good gifts to your children, how much more will the heavenly Father give the Holy Spirit to those who ask him? (Luke 11:9-13)

In this passage where Matthew has "give good gifts" Luke has "give the Holy Spirit," and it seems that Luke has edited the text in the light of one of his own favorite themes. Indeed what good gift can be better than the Holy Spirit if it is believed that the Holy Spirit will do all that he did in the apostolic age?

So in the synoptic tradition there are these powerful injunctions to make requests in prayer, and as powerful promises that prayer will be answered. But the context of the Kingdom and the Will of the Father is present. So the tension between what Christian disciples may desire and what lies within God's purpose is a tension ever continuing, and we may find an answer in the teaching in the fourth gospel about praying "in the name of Jesus."

It is clear however to readers of the gospels that just as the prayer of Jesus is a part of his whole relation to the Father in the obedience of his mission, so the prayer of the disciples is not a verbal utterance or a movement of the heart separable from the quest of righteousness. The relationship of the children to the Father includes within itself the whole range of human attitudes and activities. The beatitudes in the Sermon on the Mount describe the blessedness of those whose lives are linked with God in poverty of spirit, in hunger and thirst for righteousness, in purity of heart, in peace-making and in the endurance of persecution. To love one's enemies is to be sons of the Father, and to strive to perfection is to be in converse with the Father who is perfect. The second great commandment lies within the true practice of the first. This interpretation of prayer and loving obedience is to find powerful expression in St. Paul's words "Do all in the name of the Lord Jesus," and in the Johannine picture of the glorifying of the Father in the living and dying of Jesus and the disciples.

Meanwhile stern warnings are given about a false separation between devotion and obedience.

Why do you call me "Lord, Lord," and do not what I tell you? (Luke 6:46)

A woman in the crowd raised her voice and said to him, "Blessed is the woman that bore you, and the breasts that you sucked." But he said, "Blessed rather are those who hear the word of God and keep it." (Luke 11:27-28)

Devotion to Jesus himself is indeed evoked by his mission. But Jesus discourages a devotion which is likely to miss both ethical depth and the realization that his concern is with the Father, and the Father's kingdom. But when Jesus has died and risen again, there will be a devotion to him that is deepened by the cross and linked truly with the Father's purpose.

Meanwhile in the course of his ministry before the crucifixion Jesus has sown the seeds of what is to become the prayer of Christian people down through the centuries. The seed was there but not the flowering. Before that can come there will be the disclosure of the deepest meaning of God's kingdom or sovereignty in the death and resurrection of Jesus, and there will be also the mission of the Holy Spirit by whose power the disciples will pray *"Abba,* Father."

One piece of teaching about prayer within the synoptic gospels seems to forecast or belong to the post-resurrection setting of the Christian Church. In Matthew 18 there is a group of sayings about the life and discipline of the *ecclesia,* and among them is this saying:

Again I say to you, if two of you agree on earth about anything they ask, it will be done for them by my Father in heaven. For where two or three are gathered in my name, there am I in the midst of them. (Matthew 18:19-20)

Here the promise that prayer will be granted is linked with the gathering of disciples in the name of Jesus and the presence of Jesus in their midst. These are themes whose meaning the fourth gospel will specially draw out.

Chapter 3

The Prayer of St. Paul

I n the years which followed the resurrection of Jesus and the outpouring of the Holy Spirit on the day of Pentecost, Christians were a community in which the notes of prayer and praise were again and again sounding. If the author of Acts speaks as one for whom prayer and praise are a cherished theme, the picture there given is corroborated by the contemporary evidence of St. Paul's letters. The Christians are "those who in every place call on the name of Our Lord Jesus Christ" (1 Corinthians 1:2) and while the praying is, as we shall see, set in the midst of thanksgiving, St. Paul can describe it as an "agonizing" conflict (Colossians 2:1), a word which recalls both the wrestling of Jacob and the prayer in Gethsemane.

Amidst the prayer of the early Christians we ask what has happened to the great themes of the Lord's Prayer: the Father and the Kingdom. We find that the phrase "the Father" has a new widespread prominence, whether as the Father of Jesus or the Father of the Christians in their adopted sonship, or simply as the Father. As to "the Kingdom," the word so prominent in the synoptic tradition, we find that it is seldom used in St. Paul's letters; but God's sovereignty is strongly affirmed in other ways. Fatherhood and sovereignty are the continuing background of Christian prayer as St. Paul understands it.

Father. Saul of Tarsus would as a Jew have prayed to God as Father, invoking the creator to whom awe and reverence are given and the Father of Israel who cares for the people in righteousness and compassion. Now as a Christian he finds the word revivified for him. He prays *Abba,* using the word that was on the lips of Jesus, and he says that the Christians pray thus by the power of the Holy Spirit praying within them. "When we cry *Abba,* Father, it is the Spirit himself bearing witness to our spirits that we are children of God." So praying, St. Paul has an intimacy with God as Father which he expresses in three different phrases which recur in his letters:

God is "Our Father."
God is "the Father of Jesus Christ."
God is simply "the Father."

It is the third of these phrases which is perhaps the most telling, coming as it does in the initial greeting in several of the letters.

Kingdom, the other key word in the Lord's Prayer, is used little in St. Paul's writings; indeed the phrase "the Kingdom of God," which is so prominent in the gospel tradition, is comparatively rare in the other books of the New Testament. The phrase thus seems to belong specially to Jesus' own ministry, and after his death and resurrection prominence is now given to the Lordship of Jesus himself risen from the dead and to the Father himself revealed now in a new intimacy. When "Kingdom of God" comes in St. Paul's letters it sometimes refers to a future vindication, and sometimes to a present realization. God has called the

Christians into his eternal kingdom and glory in the day when Jesus returns (1 Thessalonians 2:12), but meanwhile the Kingdom of God is found to be here already in righteousness and joy and peace in the Holy Spirit (Romans 14:17).

While however the phrase "Kingdom of God" is infrequent in St. Paul's letters it is clear that the divine sovereignty is powerfully present in the world through Jesus himself in his death and resurrection. Christ crucified is himself the power of God and the wisdom of God, and the Gospel of Christ is the power of God into salvation. St. Paul's conviction of the divine sovereignty present in the world is reflected in his use of the word "power" applied to the Holy Spirit, to the preaching of the Gospel and to the lives of Christians. This sovereignty is sure even in face of the sufferings and frustrations of the world and of the Christians in the world. Nowhere is this more strongly expressed than at the end of the eighth chapter of the letter to the Romans.

> Who shall separate us from the love of Christ? Shall tribulation, or distress, or persecution, or famine, or nakedness, or peril, or the sword?...No, in all these things we are more than conquerors through him who loved us. For I am sure that neither death, nor life, nor angels, nor principalities, nor things present, nor things to come, nor powers, nor height, nor depth, nor anything else in all creation, will be able to separate us from the love of God in Christ Jesus our Lord. (Romans 8:35-39)

The sovereignty of God is linked with the conviction about Jesus expressed in the words "Jesus is Lord." The linking of divine sovereignty and the Lordship of Jesus is powerfully expressed in Philippians 2.

> Therefore God has highly exalted him and bestowed on him the name which is above every name, that at the name of Jesus every knee should bow, in heaven and on earth and under the earth, and every tongue confess that Jesus Christ is Lord, to the glory of God the Father. (Philippians 2:9-11)

So there is in St. Paul's mind a deep conviction of God's Fatherhood and sovereignty which colors Christian prayer, and in this way the themes of the Lord's Prayer come into their own. And there is another word, which comes into its own as well, the word **Name.**

The Name of God has meant in the ancient scriptures the reality and character of God as he revealed himself. It was the mission of Jesus to act in the name of God, that is with his character and authority, and to be revealing that character and authority. Jesus fulfills this role in such a way that his own name, the name of Jesus, came very near to the name of God. So the name of Jesus is prominent in the life of the Christian Church. Christians call upon his name (1 Corinthians 1:2). They are gathered together in his name (Matthew 18:20). They suffer for his name (Acts 5:40). They must do everything in his name (Colossians 3:17). They pray in his name, and to pray in the name of Jesus means to pray not only invoking the word Jesus but submitting to his will and purpose as Lord.

With this background of conviction it is not surprising that St. Paul prayed often with boldness and perseverance. Some of his prayers come at the beginning and the end of his letters to the various churches, and they take the form of invoking upon his readers grace and peace from the Father, and from Jesus Christ. Frequent also are prayers for the perseverance of the Christians and their growth in grace and in knowledge. But sometimes St. Paul prays for more specific wishes. He prays that he may one day be allowed to come to Rome (Romans 1:10). He prays that the nation of Israel may come to find salvation (Romans 10:1). He prays that a door may be opened for him for the power of the Gospel even when he is in prison (Colossians 4:3). He exhorts his readers not seldom to pray for him, as he prays for them; and he sees prayer as a cooperation with God's power which can be powerful in its results, telling the Philippians, "I know that through your prayers and the help of the Spirit of Jesus Christ this will turn out for my deliverance" (Philippians 1:19).

In one unusual passage St. Paul tells of an exalted experience of communion with God and this leads to a mention of his own physical illness and to his prayer concerning it. The passage is in 2 Corinthians 12, and it has great interest for St. Paul's biography as well as for the study of prayer. Mentioning "visions and revelations of the Lord," St. Paul writes:

> I know a man in Christ who fourteen years ago was caught up to the third heaven—whether in the body or out of the body I do not know, God knows. And I know that this man was caught up into Paradise— whether in the body or out of the body I do not know, God knows—and he heard things that cannot be told, which man may not utter. (2 Corinthians 12:2-4)

We cannot be sure what is the experience here described, but it may resemble what a later age would call mystical experience. But he realizes that he is wrong in trying to describe it and still more wrong if he boasts about it. But God has his answer and St. Paul continues:

> And to keep me from being too elated by the abundance of revelations, a thorn was given me in the flesh, a messenger of Satan, to harass me, to keep me from being too elated. Three times I besought the Lord about this, that it should leave me; but he said to me, "My grace is sufficient for you, for my power is made perfect in weakness." I will all the more gladly boast of my weaknesses, that the power of Christ may rest upon me. For the sake of Christ, then, I am content with weaknesses, insults, hardships, persecutions, and calamities; for when I am weak, then I am strong. (2 Corinthians 12:7-10)

The thorn in the flesh, the physical malady from which St. Paul recurringly suffered, is here seen as a lesson in humility. The prayer for its removal is not granted, but it leads to a deep reliance upon God's power, realized in weakness. Here indeed is a prayer which catches something of the spirit of Gethsemane.

Not surprisingly the note of thanksgiving resounds in St. Paul's letters. He sees the Christian life as penetrated by thanksgiving again and again. Thanksgiving is enjoined for all times and for all things (1 Thessalonians 5:17; 2 Thessalonians 2:13; Philippians 4:6; Colossians 3:15; Ephesians 5:26). It is linked with all eating and drinking (1 Corinthians 10:12) and it distinguishes true religion from false (Romans 1:25). St. Paul begins most of his letters with an outburst of thanksgiving, and the striking examples are the two Thessalonian letters, the first Corinthian letter, and the letter to Philippi. Finally the letter to the Colossians and the letter to the Ephesians begin with a pattern of thanksgiving on a large canvas, in which the needs of the Christians of the world are set in the context of the praise of God as creator and savior. In those two letters the thanksgivings have an almost liturgical kind of rhythm. The outbursts of thanksgiving belong to a communion with God which has the glory of God as its motive. Far from being a purely Johannine theme the glorifying of God belongs widely to the first age of Christianity, and St. Paul's letters give evidence of this. Significantly he tells of the giving glory to God both in utterances of doxology (e.g. Romans 11:33-35, 16:25-27; Ephesians 3:20-21) and in the everyday actions of Christian life. "So, whether you eat or drink, or whatever you do, do all to the glory of God" (1 Corinthians 10:31).

So we learn from St. Paul how the great themes of the Lord's Prayer prevail in the prayer of the early Christians. As the apostolic age proceeds a Trinitarian pattern in prayer becomes apparent. Prayer is to the Father, and Jesus is not only the one through whom the Christians pray but one who himself evokes a devotion which would be idolatrous if he were not indeed divine. It is the Spirit who enables the Christians to pray *"Abba,* Father" and to acknowledge the Lordship of Jesus. Experiencing a threefold relation to God in their prayer, the Christians are encountering a threefold relation within God himself, and the discourse and prayer in John begin to unveil this. It is within the Trinitarian character of Christian prayer that the theology of the Trinity is growing.

Chapter 4

Light from St. John

I n our study of the prayer of Jesus and the teaching
given to the disciples use was not made of the fourth
gospel as a historical source, for while that gospel
seems to draw upon early traditions it is chiefly significant
as an interpretation of the experience and theology of
Christians in the apostolic age. Not least does this gospel
throw much light upon the understanding of Christian
prayer.

The theme of prayer in the name of Jesus comes into
prominence in this gospel, and this is shown to be the
prayer of those who are closely united to Jesus by the
coming of the Holy Spirit, the Paraclete. It is thus after the
death and resurrection of Jesus that the deepest prayer of
the disciples is made possible. The prayer of Jesus to the
Father is seen in this gospel as the expression in time and
history of the Son's eternal relation to the Father, a relation
which is supremely revealed in the self-giving love of the
Passion. While this teaching about prayer lifts us into an
eternal world it does so by confronting us with the particular time and place of an event on the Hill of Calvary. In
these ways we learn about prayer much that is distinctive

in this gospel, but what we learn is rooted in the early tradition about the prayer of Jesus as his obedience even unto death.

Here are references to the prayer of Jesus in the fourth gospel. Jesus at the grave of Lazarus thanks the Father for the answering of his prayer, and he does so audibly to show that his prayer is drawn from the Father's will and purpose and his own closeness to that will and purpose.

> Father, I thank thee that thou hast heard me. I knew that thou hearest me always, but I have said this on account of the people standing by, that they may believe that thou didst send me. (John 11:41-42)

William Temple's comment is unsurpassed:

> Before the word of command the Lord, for the sake of the bystanders, utters aloud his constant thanksgiving for the Father's unfailing answer to his prayer. We are not told of any prayer, there was no wonderful moment of prayer; he lived in prayer, and doubtless was in prayer from the time when the message of the sisters reached him. Now for a moment he reveals his prayer and the assurance that it was answered.

Another occasion is in the city of Jerusalem when some Greeks approach desiring to see him, and the response of Jesus is to speak about his coming death. Aware that death is coming he asks in a moment of anguish that the hour may pass from him; and then immediately recalls that it is for this hour that he has come, and he asks that the Father will glorify his own name through the Son's obedience. Here indeed in a Johannine setting is a glimpse of the theme and spirit of the prayer in Gethsemane, and the prayer and the answer are audible that the people may know that the death of Jesus belongs to God's glory and is neither a defeat nor self-chosen martyrdom.

"Now is my soul troubled. And what shall I say? 'Father, save me from this hour'? No, for this purpose I have come to this hour. Father, glorify thy name." Then there came a voice from heaven, "I have glorified it, and I will glorify it again." (John 12:27-28)

We pass on to the supper. In the discourse Jesus speaks of the new relationship of the disciples to himself and to the Father which will be coming after his own departure and the sending of the Paraclete. Within this new order their prayers will be granted if they are made "in my name." Jesus had spoken earlier of his coming in the Father's name, and to act in someone's name is to be utterly in tune with his mind and will. So to pray in the name of Jesus is to pray with heart and mind attuned to the will of Jesus. No doubt the disciples could hardly begin to pray in the name of Jesus before his mission had been completed and the Paraclete had guided them. "Hitherto you have asked nothing in my name."

In the discourse Jesus speaks about prayer in three short passages.

The first passage follows the promise that the disciples, as a result of his departure to the Father, will do even greater works than Jesus has done.

Whatever you ask in my name, I will do it, that the Father may be glorified in the Son; if you ask anything in my name, I will do it. (John 14:13-14)

Here is a new factor: it will be Jesus himself who does what the prayer requests, and it will be done for the glorifying of the Father.

The second passage follows the description of the union of Jesus and the disciples in the imagery of the vine and the branches.

> If you abide in me, and my words abide in you, ask whatever you will, and it shall be done for you. By this my Father is glorified, that you bear much fruit, and so prove to be my disciples. (John 15:7-8)

Here the condition for prayer to be answered is described in deep terms as abiding in Jesus and letting the words of his teaching abide in the heart and mind. These phrases illuminate the meaning of praying in the name.

The third passage comes when Jesus has passed on to speak urgently about "that day," the new order now imminent.

> In that day you will ask nothing of me. Truly, truly, I say to you, if you ask anything of the Father, he will give it you in my name. Hitherto you have asked nothing in my name; ask, and you will receive, that your joy may be full. (John 16:23-24)

In the first sentence the words "you will ask nothing of me" probably mean not "you will make no requests" but rather "you will ask me no questions." The disciples have indeed often questioned Jesus in the past, and there have been several questionings of him in perplexity at the Supper, but the time is now coming when they will learn not by question and answer but by their close union with him and the guidance of his Spirit. They will have the closest access to the Father. In the name of Jesus, the Father will answer them. With the mission of Jesus on earth now ended there will be a beginning of that union with him whereby they shall ask in his name.

Is there a baffling contrast between the teaching of prayer in the name in this discourse and the exhortations to make requests which we saw in the earlier gospel tradition—"Ask and you shall receive, seek and you shall find, knock and it shall be opened to you"—as well as in the parables of the Friend at Midnight and the Widow and the Judge? There is indeed a contrast, but not a baffling one. God would have us ask for the things which belong to his own will and purpose, but he would have us ask with desires of our own and ideas of our own. He would have us bring our longings to him, but when our longings are not granted it may be that the longing is for the wrong thing or that he is testing our faith and leading us to learn the difference between faith in God and confidence in our own judgment. It has been quaintly yet fairly said: "Prayer is the medium which God has given us to induce him to desire what we desire; but it must also be the medium by which we ask him to induce us to desire what he desires." But the conflict which may be in the souls of those who pray is a conflict in which Jesus has shared, as we learn from Gethsemane and from the episode "Father, save me from this hour."

After the discourse there comes the prayer of Jesus in John 17. It has been called the High Priestly Prayer, but a more appropriate title might be the Prayer of Consecration, for at its center Jesus consecrates himself to his death on behalf of the disciples. But the recurring theme of the prayer is glory: glory in the Passion, glory given to the disciples, glory in the goal of heaven. It is a prayer set in the context of a historical situation, a place, a time, an hour, the hour of the death of Jesus in Jerusalem. Yet within the prayer there is reflected the timeless converse of the Son and the Father in a glory before the world began.

As the prayer in Gethsemane was in Mark's gospel the decisive step to the Passion, so in John this prayer after the Supper is the decisive step of Jesus towards the completion of the journey to the Father which is his mission. The Cross is the event of glory. By it there is the revelation of eternal glory, and from it there comes the mission of the disciples, their consecration in the truth, their sharing in the unity of the Father and the Son and their coming to the glory in heaven.

The prayer is in three parts. The first part is about Jesus himself, the second is about the disciples, and the third is about those who will come to be disciples through the disciples' mission.

When Jesus had spoken these words, he lifted up his eyes to heaven and said, "Father, the hour has come; glorify thy Son that the Son may glorify thee, since thou hast given him power over all flesh, to give eternal life to all whom thou hast given him. And this is eternal life, that they know thee the only true God, and Jesus Christ whom thou hast sent. I glorified thee on earth, having accomplished the work which thou gavest me to do; and now, Father, glorify thou me in thy own presence with the glory which I had with thee before the world was made.

"I have manifested thy name to the men whom thou gavest me out of the world; thine they were, and thou gavest them to me, and they have kept thy word. Now they know that everything that thou hast given me is from thee; for I have given them the

words which thou gavest me, and they have received them and know in truth that I came from
thee; and they have believed that thou didst send
me. I am praying for them; I am not praying for the
world but for those whom thou hast given me, for
they are thine; all mine are thine, and thine are
mine, and I am glorified in them. And now I am no
more in the world, but they are in the world, and I
am coming to thee. Holy Father, keep them in thy
name, which thou hast given me, that they may be
one, even as we are one. While I was with them, I
kept them in thy name, which thou hast given me; I
have guarded them, and none of them is lost but the
son of perdition, that the scripture might be fulfilled.
But now I am coming to thee; and these things I
speak in the world, that they may have my joy fulfilled in themselves. I have given them thy word; and
the world has hated them because they are not of
the world, even as I am not of the world. I do not
pray that thou shouldst take them out of the world,
but that thou shouldst keep them from the evil one.
They are not of the world, even as I am not of the
world. Sanctify them in the truth; thy word is truth.
As thou didst send me into the world, so I have sent
them into the world. And for their sake I consecrate
myself, that they also may be consecrated in truth.

"I do not pray for these only, but also for those who
believe in me through their word, that they may all
be one; even as thou, Father, art in me, and I in thee,
that they also may be in us, so that the world may
believe that thou hast sent me. The glory which thou
hast given me I have given to them that they may be
one even as we are one, I in them and thou in me,

that they may become perfectly one, so that the world may know that thou hast sent me and hast loved them even as thou hast loved me. Father, I desire that they also, whom thou hast given me, may be with me where I am, to behold my glory which thou hast given me in thy love for me before the foundation of the world. O righteous Father, the world has not known thee, but I have known thee; and these know that thou hast sent me. I made known to them thy name, and I will make it known, that the love with which thou hast loved me may be in them, and I in them." (John 17:1-26)

Verses 1-5: Jesus prays that in the event of the next day the Father may give glory to him and he may give glory to the Father, by showing in the crucifixion the self-giving love which is the secret of glory from eternity. The act of glorifying will be in virtue of the power of Jesus over mankind, a power to be seen in the bestowal of eternal life to those who are his own (the evangelist inserts here his description of eternal life as the knowledge of the Father and the Son). Jesus has already glorified the Father in his life on earth and may he now be glorified with the Father's presence in an act which manifests glory from the eternal love.

Verses 6-19: Jesus has made the Father known to the disciples whom the Father has given to him, and they have received the revelation and kept it fast. But now they are being left in the world, and he prays that they may be kept faithful to the revelation given to them and that they may be consecrated in the truth. For their sake Jesus is consecrating himself to the truth. The disciples are required to be not of this world in two ways. As I wrote in *The Glory of God,* the disciples are to be consecrated to God in opposition to the world's self-pleasing; they are to represent the truth of God in opposition to the world's errors. The two requirements are inseparable, even as grace and truth are inseparable in the mission of Christ. Lack of consecration may corrupt their witness to the truth, and woolliness of mind concerning the truth entrusted to them may betray them into a facile assimilation of the world's own presuppositions. Therefore Jesus prays, "Sanctify them in the truth." There is no holiness apart from the theology which he reveals, and there is no imparting of the theology except by consecrated lives.

Verses 20-26: The theme of unity now appears. Jesus prays for the unity of all the future believers. This unity is not just a fellowship among themselves but a unity in the Father and in the Son, in a way that resembles the Father being in the Son and the Son being in the Father. This will happen by the giving to them of the glory, the glory which comes from eternity and is revealed in the Passion. This indwelling of the glory in the believers will vindicate the Son's mission and the Father's love. Finally, the prayer moves towards heaven. Jesus wills that the disciples may be with him where he is and may have the vision of glory. Then the prayer moves down to earth again with the thought of the presence of the disciples in an unbelieving and unknowing world. May they be kept in the love of the Father for Jesus and for them.

Be still and know: uttered on earth as all the prayers of Jesus were, they belong to heaven, to eternity. It is from heaven and eternity that our own power to pray is drawn.

Chapter 5

Through the Veil

Deep in the Christian tradition is the belief that the prayer of Jesus is ever continuing. He who prayed on the Mount of Transfiguration and in the Garden of Gethsemane and on the Hill of Calvary still prays. The imagery of Jesus as the ceaseless intercessor has deeply influenced Christian worship and spirituality throughout the centuries. We have to ask what the idea means and how we may understand it today.

That Jesus is risen and alive is one of the central convictions of Christianity, and he lives as the one who once died for the sins of the world. In our approach to him today as one who is alive, we confront his death in its moral relation to ourselves. But while that death was a costly necessity for the redemption of the world it has within it the Father's self-giving love, for "God commends his own love towards us in that Christ died for us" (Romans 5:8) and "God was in Christ reconciling the world to himself" (2 Corinthians 5:19). So too the prayer of Jesus in heaven is no pleading to an estranged or hostile Father. Each of the writers who tells of the intercession or advocacy in heaven tells no less of the divine initiative of love. But it cost and it costs, and the costliness belongs to the imagery of sacrifice on earth and of intercession in heaven.

Three kinds of imagery are mingled concerning the risen and ascended life of Jesus. He is with the Father as the perfect sacrifice, as the victor over evil (the image of sitting at the right hand of God) and as the intercessor; and it is within this complex of images that the verb translated "intercede" has its place.

St. Paul refers to the intercession of Jesus in the eighth chapter of the letter to the Romans:

> It is God who justifies; who is to condemn? Is it Christ Jesus, who died, yes, who was raised from the dead, who is at the right hand of God, who indeed intercedes for us? (Romans 8:33-34)

We notice the context in which the interceding is set: it is God's generosity in the giving of his own Son, and in the justifying of sinners, and it is also the sovereignty of Jesus "at the right hand of God."

The imagery of intercession is, in the Epistle to the Hebrews, near to the central theme of the book. Here the context is the priesthood of Christ in heaven and the imagery of offering is blended with the imagery of reigning in power, and this imagery is the background to the new approach to God of those who respond to what God has done for them through Christ.

> The former priests were many in number, because they were prevented by death from continuing in office; but he holds his priesthood permanently, because he continues for ever. Consequently he is able for all time to save those who draw near to God through him, since he always lives to make intercession for them. (Hebrews 7:23-25)

In citing these passages we have used the verb "intercede" which in English versions of the New Testament is used in translation of the Greek verb. But the translation "intercede" is liable to misunderstanding. The Greek verb does not properly mean to speak or to plead or to make petitions or entreaties; it means rather to be with someone, to meet or encounter someone, in relation to others. What is called the intercession of Jesus means his ceaseless presence with the Father. He is with the Father not as begging the Father to be gracious, for from the Father graciousness ever flows. He is with the Father as one who once died for us on Calvary; with the Father in the presence of a life which is ever, the life that died; with the Father as one who was tempted as we are and bore our sins and our sufferings; with the Father as the focus of our hopes and desires. To approach the Father through Jesus Christ the intercessor is to approach in awareness of the cost of our redemption by a sacrifice made once for all and a victory once accomplished, a sacrifice and victory which are both past history and ever present realities. It is this which both enables and characterizes our response to God through Jesus Christ.

We now turn to the account of the response of Christian believers to the sacrifice and victory of Christ as drawn out in the Epistle to the Hebrews. It is worth our while to do this as no writer depicts the response in such varied and vivid ways.

The epistle was written by an unknown author to an unknown Christian community which was in grave crisis through the danger of backsliding from Christian loyalty. It is not certain that it was a community of Jewish Christians who might be lapsing into Judaism; it may have been a predominantly Gentile Christian community which was finding the Christian faith so hard a struggle that the temptation was to slip into apathy and to give up the effort of Christianity. The writer sets out to show that issues of finality, of life and death are at stake, for the end is near. Jesus Christ is final, and is the universal savior of mankind; and the Christian claim is unshaken as true for all men and for all time. This finality of Christ is expressed in the imagery of priesthood. "Think of Jesus as priest," the writer seems to say, "and you will understand how universal and imperative is his claim." His sacrifice is the key to reality. So do not drift away, but draw near in faith.

The response is described in vivid language: "draw near," "the new and living way," "through the veil," "you are come to Mount Zion," "we have here no continuing city but we seek a city which is to come," "go out to Jesus bearing his reproach." It has been the mission of Jesus to open the way for mankind, and two aspects of this mission are described. On the one hand Jesus is the divine son in the revelation of God to mankind. On the other hand it is a special theme of Hebrews that Jesus in his identification with mankind pioneers the way for himself and for us along the road of faith towards the goal.

Jesus has led the way. In chapter two we learn that it has been his mission to bring many sons to glory and to that end he is utterly fitted by the sufferings he bore, being made like unto his brethren; suffering and tempted he is fitted to be mankind's priest. He passes through the heavens. He goes before us as our forerunner. He has opened for us a new and living way. He is the beginner and the completer of our faith. In achieving this he was indeed utterly rejected and suffered outside the gate, and we are called to go out to him and bear his reproach. He is indeed the way.

It is by the sacrifice of Jesus, in the flesh and blood of history and in its presence in heaven, that the way is opened. The transition is made, from the victory of Christ to the believers' response, in the middle of chapter ten. By the offering of his obedient will to death Jesus has once for all set in the true and perfect relation to God those who are now being sanctified.

Here are some of the passages which describe the response, and which together in their varied imagery illuminate the character of the Christian life.

> Therefore, brethren, since we have confidence to enter the sanctuary by the blood of Jesus, by the new and living way which he opened for us through the curtain, that is, through his flesh, and since we have a great priest over the house of God, let us draw near with a true heart in full assurance of faith, with our hearts sprinkled clean from an evil conscience and our bodies washed with pure water. Let us hold fast the confession of our hope without wavering, for he who promised is faithful; and let us consider how to stir up one another to love and good works, not neglecting to meet together, as is the habit of some, but encouraging one another, and all the more as you see the Day drawing near. (Hebrews 10:19-25)

The curtain or veil is from the imagery of the tabernacle, prominent in this epistle; it hangs between the holy place and the holy of holies, and it has been a symbol of the frontier between earth and heaven. Through the veil there is now an open way, which is Jesus himself. He is the way, walk in it. Cleansed by the waters of baptism and freed from the burdens of bad conscience we may draw near.

But in drawing near we do not leave behind the urgent practical duties of Christian life, indeed we turn to them more vigorously: to compassion, good works, fellowship and the meeting together. It is urgent and the time is short.

There follows a passage of urgent and terrible warning. To fail to respond is to slip into apostasy and a kind of apostasy which means the repudiating of our privileges, the blaspheming of the blood of Jesus and the crucifying of him afresh. There can be no renewal if such apostasy occurs. But let it not be so, says the writer. Remember your firm faithfulness under the persecution and imitate your past leaders. It is faith that is needed, and faith is to lay hold on unseen realities (Hebrews 10:26–11:1).

There follows the great chapter eleven concerning faith, and its context is the urgent response of the believers through the new and living way. Faith is not defined so much as illustrated and described in these words:

> Now faith is the assurance of things hoped for, the conviction of things not seen. (Hebrews 11:1)

There follows the recalling of many heroes of faith in the old covenant. In every case they were men who, living in this world, grasped the reality of things unseen and so reached out towards the heavenly country. At the end of the series of faith's heroes of old time there comes Jesus the supreme exemplar of faith.

> Therefore, since we are surrounded by so great a cloud of witnesses, let us also lay aside every weight, and sin which clings so closely, and let us run with perseverance the race that is set before us, looking to Jesus the pioneer and perfecter of our faith, who for the joy that was set before him endured the cross, despising the shame, and is seated

at the right hand of the throne of God. (Hebrews 12:1-2)

The next description of the response comes a little later and with different imagery.

> You have not come to what may be touched, a blazing fire, and darkness, and gloom, and a tempest, and the sound of a trumpet, and a voice whose words made the hearers entreat that no further messages be spoken to them. For they could not endure the order that was given, "If even a beast touches the mountain, it shall be stoned." Indeed, so terrifying was the sight that Moses said, "I tremble with fear." But you have come to Mount Zion and to the city of the living God, the heavenly Jerusalem, and to innumerable angels in festal gathering, and to the assembly of the firstborn who are enrolled in heaven, and to a judge who is God of all, and to the spirits of just men made perfect, and to Jesus, the mediator of a new covenant, and to the sprinkled blood that speaks more graciously than the blood of Abel. (Hebrews 12:18-24)

Here the theme is still the journey heavenward. But the arrival is described. And there is the contrast between Mount Sinai, with its darkness and terror, and the heavenly Jerusalem, where the Christians have arrived, to join in fellowship with the angels and the saints, who are at first the saints of the old covenant. But warning follows in the next verses. The end is near, with a convulsion of the universe, yet from the convulsion there will remain an unshakeable kingdom. Receive it, for it is for you, knowing that God is still the God who evokes reverence and awe. It is a distorted Christianity which in the midst of the joy of the heavenly journey forgets the awe and the dread. "There-fore let us be grateful for receiving a kingdom that cannot be shaken, and thus let us offer to God acceptable wor-ship, with reverence and awe; for our God is a consuming fire" (Hebrews 12:28-29).

The third passage about the response is a blending of images.

> The bodies of those animals whose blood is brought into the sanctuary by the high priest as a sacrifice for sin are burned outside the camp. So Jesus also suf-fered outside the gate in order to sanctify the people through his own blood. Therefore let us go forth to him outside the camp, bearing abuse for him. For here we have no lasting city, but we seek the city which is to come. Through him then let us continu-ally offer up a sacrifice of praise to God, that is, the fruit of lips that acknowledge his name. Do not ne-glect to do good and to share what you have, for such sacrifices are pleasing to God. (Hebrews 13:11-16)

In the old sin offerings, the body of the animal was not eaten but was destroyed outside the encampment. So, too, Jesus utterly rejected was put to death outside the city. Go out to him, that is the summons to Christians, go out to him and share his reproach and rejection. Our lasting city is not here, for it is a city yet to come. The Christian life means saying goodbye to the world's securities and being ready for rejection. But this otherworldly calling includes the practical life of Christian fellowship. Do good, show compassion, live in fellowship, offer worship, these are the sacrifices which God expects, united as they are with Je-sus on Calvary and Jesus in heaven. It is in the midst of the practicalities of this life that the otherworldly calling is realized.

Amidst the writings of the New Testament, the Epistle to the Hebrews often seems very remote from us in its language and its cultural setting. But it can speak to us still with a powerful message about the things which are not shaken. The imagery of holding on to a reality which is unseen can mean much amidst the meaningless chaos of the world which we do see. The theme of faith as seeing one who is invisible may mean much to some to whom the Pauline or Johannine imagery of Christ-in-us may be puzzling. So, too, the message that security is not to be found in any of the world's structures, can evoke a response in these times, with the warning against identifying Christianity with any one of its cultural forms in this world. Finally, while the response is "through the veil" and Christianity is uncompromisingly otherworldly, it is never a flight from that sacrificial existence in this world where Christians worship and have fellowship with one another. It is in the Christlike and the sacrificial that reality is to be found.

Chapter 6

The Mount
and the Plain

T he story of the Transfiguration of Jesus on the mountain has had its impact upon Christian spirituality through the centuries. It is a story of symbols—the Light, the Witnesses, the Cloud, and the Voice—symbols which speak to us still. While Mark and Matthew present the scene as a picture in itself, Luke, as was often his way, links the scene with the prayer of Jesus and the spiritual journey of Jesus towards his death. But in all of the accounts the episode is linked with other themes of the Gospel. The voice saying "This is my son" recalls the baptism of Jesus in Jordan, the note of time "after six days" links the event with the recent prediction by Jesus of his suffering and death, the radiant light tells of the glory at the future coming of Jesus, and the presence of Moses and Elijah recalls the age-long purpose of God in the scriptures.

Here is Mark's account.

After six days Jesus took with him Peter and James and John, and led them up a high mountain apart by themselves; and he was transfigured before them, and his garments became glistening, intensely white, as no fuller on earth could bleach them. And there appeared to them Elijah with Moses; and they were talking to Jesus. And Peter said to Jesus, "Master, it is well that we are here; let us make three booths, one for you and one for Moses and one for Elijah." For he did not know what to say, for they were exceedingly afraid. And a cloud overshadowed them, and a voice came out of the cloud, "This is my beloved son; listen to him." And suddenly looking around they no longer saw any one with them but Jesus only. (Mark 9:2-8)

We notice the series of symbols. First the three disciples see Jesus surrounded by intense white radiance, a radiance which Mark quaintly says could not be manufactured by any fuller on earth. The radiance is a vision of Jesus as he would be when he returns in glory. The comment of St. Basil is true to the meaning: "Peter and the sons of thunder saw his beauty on the mountain, outshining the brightness of the sun, and they were deemed worthy to receive the anticipation of his glorious parousia with their eyes." Jesus is seen in glory in spite of the coming suffering and death. One day it would be known that the glory is not in spite of the suffering and death, but in its very midst. But that day had not yet come.

Two figures are now seen, and somehow the disciples know that they are Moses and Elijah. There were traditions that some of the heroes of Israel's past would reappear when the day of the Lord was imminent, and the sight would say to the disciples that indeed the day of fulfillment was at last at hand. Moses and Elijah also stand for Law and Prophecy and these bear their witness to the

Messiah. Presently they disappear, their work has been fulfilled and Jesus stands alone.

Then Simon Peter responds to the bewildering scene,
and in what he says he is, as so often, wonderfully right
and utterly wrong. It is good indeed that the disciples
should be here with Jesus, not least when Jesus is in glory.
It is good indeed to offer a little service to Jesus and the
two witnesses, so that they may have shelter on the mountain and may stay. So courteous is Peter, and perceptive
also, for he may be thinking of the tradition which links the
coming of the day of the Lord with the Feast of Taberna-
cles, symbolizing the Lord tabernacling with his people.
But how wrong he is. Moses and Elijah are going and not
staying, and Jesus will not be lingering on the mountain,
for the divine tabernacling with mankind is to happen in a
way Peter could not fathom.

The cloud appears. This is no mountain mist floating
across the scene. It is the divine presence, in the symbol
known to the Israelites in their journeying in the wilderness. The cloud says, God is here, God in mystery and
darkness, God in awe and in intimacy. Not thoughts about
God however true, but God himself, unspeakable, invisible, with all else drowned in a night of the senses. No
wonder they are afraid.

From the cloud comes the voice, telling of the sonship
of Jesus: "This is my son, hearken to him." To hearken in
biblical language means not just to listen but to hear and
obey. Whatever Jesus says to them, they must listen to and
obey, whether he says comforting things like, "Come unto
me and I will refresh you," or hard things like, "Lo, we go
up to Jerusalem and the son of man must suffer."

The symbols now cease and Jesus stands there alone.

Matthew, whose account is very similar to Mark's, puts the fear of the disciples not at the cloud but after the voice, and he tells of Jesus speaking to them and bidding them not to fear. Luke's account has fascinating features of its own, calling for our special notice. Here it is.

Now about eight days after these sayings he took with him Peter and John and James, and went up on the mountain to pray. And as he was praying, the appearance of his countenance was altered, and his raiment became dazzling white. And behold, two men talked with him, Moses and Elijah, who appeared in glory and spoke of his departure, which he was to accomplish at Jerusalem. Now Peter and those who were with him were heavy with sleep but kept awake, and they saw his glory and the two men who stood with him. And as the men were parting from him, Peter said to Jesus, "Master, it is well that we are here; let us make three booths, one for you and one for Moses and one for Elijah"—not knowing what he said. As he said this, a cloud came and overshadowed them; and they were afraid as they entered the cloud. And a voice came out of the cloud, saying, "This is my Son, my Chosen; listen to him!" And when the voice had spoken, Jesus was found alone. And they kept silence and told no one in those days anything of what they had seen. (Luke 9:28-36)

Here is Luke's characteristic relating of a scene to prayer and to the mission of Jesus as he moves towards death and glory. Jesus is praying, and the light shines on his face. We do not know that it is a prayer of agony and conflict like the prayer in Gethsemane, but we know that it is a prayer near to the radiance of God and the prayer of one who has chosen the way of death. Luke tells us that the two witnesses were conversing about the exodus which Jesus would accomplish in Jerusalem: not the death alone, but the passing through death to glory, the whole going forth of Jesus as well as the leading forth of the new people of God in the freedom of the new covenant. Luke tells us that after the resurrection Jesus spoke of the witness of Moses and of all the prophets to his suffering and glory.

It was not a glory which the disciples at the time could fathom. No doubt they would have welcomed a glory on the mountain far away from the conflicts which had happened and the conflicts which were going to happen as Jesus set his face towards Jerusalem. Yet when Jesus went up the mountain to be transfigured he did not leave these conflicts behind, but rather carried them up the mountain so that they were transfigured with him. It was the transfiguration of the whole Christ, from his first obedience in childhood right through to the final obedience of Gethsemane and Calvary.

The disciples could not grasp this at the time, but the writings of the apostolic age were to show that the link between the suffering and the glory came to be understood as belonging to the heart of the Christian message. The first epistle of Peter was written to Christians in Asia Minor who had faced persecution and were likely to face persecution still more severe, and the writer says to them: "If you are reproached with the name of Christ, you are blessed, because the Spirit of the glory and of God rests upon you." That phrase "the Spirit of the glory" is striking. James died a martyr's death at the hands of King Herod in Jerusalem; he saw the glory. John's name is linked with the gospel which depicts the passion of Jesus as glory triumphing; indeed the fourth gospel has been described as law and prophecy witnessing to the glory of Jesus with the Cross as its climax. Glory belongs to the plain as well as to the mountain.

✢

Transfiguration is indeed a central theme of Christianity, the transforming of sufferings and circumstances, of men and women with the vision of Christ before them and the Holy Spirit within them. The language both of vision and of transformation is found in the Pauline, Johannine, and Petrine writings in the New Testament, and the language tells of Christian experience which recurs through the centuries. This is not to say that there are many conscious references to the Transfiguration story in the New Testament writings, but only that the themes are recurring Christian themes and the Transfiguration is a symbol of them.

The transfiguring of suffering is attested in Christian life. Sometimes a person suffers greatly, and the suffering continues and does not disappear; but through nearness to Christ there is seen a courage, an outgoing love and sympathy, a power of prayer, a Christlikeness of a wonderful kind. It is a privilege of the Christian pastor to be meeting these experiences and to be learning from them more than he can ever teach. In the testimony to these experiences in the apostolic writings perhaps the most moving instance is near the end of chapter eight of the letter to the Romans.

Who shall separate us from the love of Christ? Shall tribulation, or distress, or persecution, or famine, or nakedness, or peril, or sword?....No, in all these things we are more than conquerors through him who loved us. (Romans 8:35,37)

I love the comment of Karl Barth on the passage:

Thus our tribulation without ceasing to be tribulation is transformed. We suffer as we suffered before, but our suffering is no longer a passive perplexity, but is transformed into a pain which is creative, fruitful, full of power and promise. The road which is impassable has been made known to us in the crucified and risen Lord.

Circumstances are transfigured. Something blocks your path, some fact of life or person or obstacle which is utterly thwarting and frustrating. It seems impossible to remove it or ignore it or surmount it. But when it is seen in a larger context, and that context is Jesus crucified and risen, it is in a new orbit of relationships and while it remains, it remains differently. A phrase of St. Paul in 2 Corinthians 4 seems to interpret the experience, when he contrasts our "light affliction" with the "exceeding weight of glory," the one belonging to time and the other to eternity. Such is the transforming of circumstances, not by their abolition but by the lifting of them into the orbit of a crucified and risen Jesus.

Central indeed is the theme of the transforming of persons. Several passages in the apostolic writings describe this in relation to the vision of Christ as the goal and the power of the Spirit within. It is too much to say that there is a conscious reference to the event of the Transfiguration but it can indeed be said that the symbolism of the event is linked with the characteristics of the Christian life. In 2 Corinthians 3, St. Paul is using allegorical imagery to contrast the old covenant of the time of Moses and the new covenant in the Gospel. The first brought condemnation, the second brings liberty. The first is linked with the passing radiance on the face of Moses, the second with an enduring light of glory which the Christians are able both to see and to reflect.

> We are all, with unveiled face, beholding the glory of the Lord, are being changed into his likeness from one degree of glory to another; for this comes from the Lord who is the Spirit. (2 Corinthians 3:11)

The Christians gaze, not indeed directly but as in a glass or mirror, upon the glory of God, for Jesus is its perfect mirror and reflection. With this vision before them they are changed into his likeness, and it is the Holy Spirit who as Lord works the change within them. Another passage about the transforming of the Christians mentions neither the vision nor the indwelling Spirit but probes deeply into the ways in which the transforming happens.

> I appeal to you therefore, brethren, by the mercies of God, to present your bodies as a living sacrifice, holy and acceptable to God, which is your spiritual worship. Do not be conformed to this world but be transformed by the renewal of your mind, that you may prove what is the will of God, what is good and acceptable and perfect. (Romans 12:1-2)

It all begins by God's own *mercy*. Responding to that mercy the apostle bids his fellow Christians offer their own lives as a sacrifice, for that is the true meaning of worship. Then there must come a radical *break with the world*; conformity to its ways and ideas must be abandoned. Refusing the conformity to the world we can then be *transformed* towards Christ, and the secret of this transforming is to be given a *new mind,* and that mind is no doubt the mind of Christ, vividly portrayed in Philippians 2 as the mind of the one who became a servant. Through the transforming and the receiving of a new mind it becomes possible to discern what is *the will of God* and what are those things describable as good and perfect. Here indeed is a searching analysis of the transforming of human lives.

In these ways the transfiguring of suffering, circumstances, and people belongs to the experience of the Christian life as well as to the apostolic teaching. But the teaching looks forward also to a transfiguring in the future. St. Paul in Colossians tells of how the present life of the Christians in union with the risen life of Jesus will have fulfillment at the coming of Christ: "When Christ who is our life appears, then you also will appear with him in glory" (Colossians 3:4). The first epistle of John tells of the present sonship of the Christians' finding fulfillment in a day when their likeness to Jesus and vision of God will be realized: "Beloved, we are God's children now; it does not yet appear what we shall be, but we know that when he appears we shall be like him, for we shall see him as he is" (1 John 3:2). Here indeed is the fulfillment of the Lord's promise, "Blessed are the pure in heart for they shall see God."

Be still and know. The scene on the mount speaks to us today, but we are not allowed to linger there. We are bidden to journey on to Calvary and there learn of the darkness and the desolation which are the cost of the glory. But from Calvary and Easter there comes a Christian hope of immense range: the hope of the transformation not only of mankind but of the cosmos too. In Eastern Christianity especially there has been the continuing belief that Easter is the beginning of a transformed cosmos.

There is indeed a glimpse of this hope in St. Paul's letter to the Romans, a hope that "the creation itself will be set free from its bondage to decay and obtain the glorious liberty of the children of God." The bringing of mankind to glory will be the prelude to the beginning of all creation. Is this hope mere fantasy? At its root there is the belief in the divine sovereignty of sacrificial love, a sovereignty made credible only by transfigured lives.

Part Two

Chapter 7

The Christian Prays

From our glimpse of Jesus praying on the hills of Galilee and in the Garden of Gethsemane we pass to a familiar sight, the Christian who prays today. It may help us if we recall the verb which the Epistle to the Hebrews uses in describing the prayer of the ascended Jesus. The verb means "to be with" or "to encounter," rather than to plead or speak or make petitions. Jesus is ever with the Father with the world upon his heart. May we think of our own prayer as being for a while consciously with the Father, no more and no less than that? If we think of prayer thus we may find that the many aspects of prayer are embraced within the act of being in God's presence.

When you have a great friend you may plan to spend a time with him and may be careful not to miss it. The use of the time is unlikely to be planned, but within the time news may be shared, requests may be made, regrets or gratitude may be spoken, and minds may be exchanged sometimes by talking and listening and sometimes with little word or gesture. The use of the time is not organized, but the time itself may be protected with care and trouble. May not our prayer be rather like that? It is the keeping of a little time in the conscious awareness of one who is friend as well as creator and savior.

To be with God for a space. Within this may be included every aspect of prayer which the textbooks have described. To be with God wondering, that is adoration. To be with God gratefully, that is thanksgiving. To be with God ashamed, that is contrition. To be with God with others on the heart that is intercession. The secret is the quest of God's presence: "Thy face Lord will I seek." We shall indeed give forethought to the ways in which the time will be spent, but the outcome may be determined not only by our designs but by God's act in shaping both the time and ourselves. Thus our prayer is not only our own action but a divine energy with us as the Spirit within us cries, *"Abba, Father."* The rhythm however is likely to pass through adoration, thanksgiving, contrition, and intercession, as we wonder, thank, confess, and find people and needs upon the heart. All unself-consciously our prayer is in the pattern of the Lord's Prayer.

Within this context a few words may be helpful about intercession and about concentration.

To intercede is to bear others on the heart in God's presence. Our own wantings have their place, for it is clear from the teaching of Jesus that God wants us to want and to tell him of our wants. When however we do this "in the name of Jesus" we learn to bend our wantings to our glimpses of the divine will. Intercession thus becomes not the bombardment of God with requests so much as the bringing of our desires within the stream of God's own compassion. Perhaps the theory of intercession may be described in this way. The compassion of God flows ceaselessly towards the world, but it seems to wait upon the cooperation of human wills. This cooperation is partly by God's creatures doing the things which God desires to be done, and partly by prayers which are also channels of God's compassion. In intercession therefore we dwell first upon the loving-kindness of God in recollection and praise and thankfulness. It is there that intercession begins, dwelling upon God's greatness and goodness and flowing from the act of worship.

Concerned as it is with the divine will, prayer is at once concerned with the Kingdom of God. We pray for the coming of the Kingdom. Its coming must needs include both the conversion of persons and the shaping of society, for persons and society react upon one another. It is a half-truth to say that the conversion of persons will put society right, and it is less than a half-truth to say, "Rectify society and the people will thereby be redeemed." There is a far deeper interweaving of these two realms. As the Christian prays for the world he must needs be facing the question, "Who is my neighbor?" That question hits him as he prays for those of other races, not least those who live within his own country, for those in poverty and hunger near or far away, for those who suffer cruelty and injustice, for those who make decisions concerning weapons which could destroy civilization. To pray with understanding is not necessarily to pray with knowledge of the answers. But it is to pray as one whom the questions move to the agony of caring and compassion.

As to concentration, there are times when prayer vibrates with joy and eagerness, and there are times when the brain seems stupider than ever, the imagination wanders far away and the feelings are cold and the will very weak. At such times it may be the best course simply to repeat acts of wanting God, of wanting to pray, of wanting to love, of wanting to have faith, not shrinking from the repetition of the phrases. To pray thus is to expose one's own weakness in God's presence and to ask him to use our little fragments of wanting and loving beyond what we ask or have. If the enthusiasm of a full heart brings us near to God, no less near to him is the prayer of a frail and sincere wanting. It may open the soul to a new pouring in of the love of God.

Not as a remedy for distraction but as a glorious prayer in its own right is the prayer known as the Jesus Prayer, used and loved by Eastern Christians for many years and lately loved increasingly by many Christians in the West. This prayer is the repetition again and again of the words "Lord Jesus Christ, Son of the Living God, have mercy upon me, a sinner." The repetition, many times and many times, is found to quieten the distracting parts of our personalities and to keep us wonderfully subdued and concentrated, and as we repeat the words again and again we bring into our heart the many people and needs about whom we really want to pray. As the words proceed the heart has the people on it one by one. To intercede need not mean to address phrases to God about this person or that, but to bear them upon the heart in God's presence.

The praying Christian is one whose prayer is uniquely his own, a divine and human movement within his own soul and nowhere else; and as no two people are the same, so the prayer of no two people is the same. But solitary as prayer may be it is always interwoven with the prayer of Jesus, the prayer of the Holy Spirit within, and the praying family of the Church in every place.

1. The prayer of Jesus is still the background and the strength of the prayers of his disciples. Today we may re-

call the scenes in the gospels where Jesus is praying and draw from them a contemporary impact. Thus the story of Gethsemane is a story about Christian disciples in any age. Jesus warned them "Watch therefore—for you do not know when the master of the house will come...—lest he come suddenly and find you asleep. And what I say to you I say to all; Watch" (Mark 13:35-36). Jesus, having thus warned the disciples when speaking to them in the temple, exhorts the three disciples in the garden to watch and pray near to him. Three times they sleep, and in the midst of his own agony he comes over to them as the loving pastor to stir them to watch and to pray. Jesus still is praying near to us, and as our loving pastor he comes to stir us to watch and to pray.

2. The prayer of the Holy Spirit is the creative link between the prayer of Jesus and the Christians who make the prayer of Jesus their own. In linking the prayer of the Christians to the prayer of Jesus the Holy Spirit enables their participation in him with one another. The phrase which is unsatisfactorily translated "the fellowship of the Holy Spirit," really means "the sharing in the Holy Spirit," and this is in a way which means also our sharing in and with one another. So St. Paul in Philippians links participation in the Holy Spirit with "having among yourselves the mind which is yours in Christ Jesus" (Philippians 2:1,5). Here indeed is a deep fulfillment of the injunction of Jesus to disciples to agree together about the object of their prayer. The vividly corporate aspect of prayer is described in Ephesians:

> Do not get drunk with wine, for that is debauchery; but be filled with the Spirit, addressing one another in psalms and hymns and spiritual songs, singing and making melody to the Lord with all your heart,

always and for everything giving thanks in the name
of our Lord Jesus Christ to God the Father. (Ephesians 5:18-20)

Thus it is that the Spirit liberates us from inhibitions in relating us to one another as we pray.

3. The praying Christian is also part of the praying
Church, however solitary he may be or feel. The praying
Church means not only a local community or the church
of a country or a generation, but the Holy Catholic Church
of Christ, the people of God in all places and all ages. Divi-
sions of place and time, of culture and of our unhappy
separations may hinder but do not destroy the unity in
Christ of those who know their prayer to be in Christ. To
say this is not to deny the solitude of the single Christian in
the uniqueness in which the creator made him. Rather
may the Christian draw from the liturgy of the worshiping
Church a strength whereby his own prayer becomes more
than ever his own in depth, enabling him in turn to bring
into the liturgy the offering of his own devotion.

The Eucharist is the supreme confrontation between
God and his redeemed people, through the recalling of the
death of Jesus. Here the people feed upon Jesus, who died
and rose again, and offer themselves to the Father in union
with his own perfect sacrifice. Into this act each Christian
brings the offering of his own prayer. From this act each
Christian draws divine strength into his own prayer in
times of quiet. It is greatly to be desired that those who
care specially for liturgy, and plan it, would give more care
to the relation between liturgy and personal prayer and
meditation. If every spare moment within and around the
liturgy is filled with music and activity much is lost in the
linking of liturgy to the meditative and contemplative aspects of the Christian life.

The Christian who is struggling with his prayers far from the visible aids of the Christian community will realize that he is never alone. Christians are praying in many parts of the world, sometimes in places where persecution and cruelty are, and their prayers are near to the Christ. The recollection of that may strengthen the prayer of the lonely Christian. So too may the bringing into personal prayer of some of the forms of common prayer, a collect, a psalm, a hymn, as a link with the praying people of God. Some of the psalms wonderfully link one who prays with the prayer of Jesus and the praying Church through the ages. Not least is this true of the rolling cadences of Psalm 119.

4. The praying Christian will not forget that the prayers of the saints are near to him. In a later chapter we shall be thinking about the Communion of Saints and the oneness of saints on earth and in paradise and in heaven. There is no need to fear that we shall be treating the saints as mediators, supplementing or replacing the unique mediation of Jesus in whose name we pray. Rather do we pray that our prayers may be helped by the prayers of other Christians who pray better than we do, and if this is true of Christians praying on earth, whether alongside us or in other parts of the world, how true it may be of the prayers of saints who are beyond the grave and nearer to the holiness of God and the vision of God in his beauty.

5. The praying Christian finally draws inspiration from the world for which he prays. Sometimes the beauty he sees in the world will stir him to wonder and to worship. Sometimes the presence of the divine word in human lives of goodness or wisdom will stir him with gratitude and reverence. The presence of self-sacrifice in human lives will set him thinking of Calvary. More often perhaps the agony of the world will draw him to the compassion of Jesus and

stir his will to pray. He will know that by their worship and prayer Christians serve the world powerfully. To worship is to recapture the truth told by St. Irenaeus: "The glory of God is a living man, the life of man is the vision of God." The role of the Christian in the world is strikingly described in the anonymous Letter to Diognetus in the second century: "As the soul is in the body so are the Christians in the world." By their praying the Christians are helping the world to recover the soul which the world has lost.

Chapter 8

Towards Contemplation

The meditative element frequently appears in Christian prayer. Both in personal prayer and in liturgy Christians will be thinking about God, however slightly, before they speak to him. Many of Cranmer's collects begin by reflecting upon some aspect of the greatness and goodness of God before we make our requests.

O God, who has prepared for them that love thee such good things as pass man's understanding....

Lord of all power and might, who art the author and giver of all good things....

Almighty and merciful God, of whose only gift it cometh that thy faithful people do unto thee true and laudable service....

Almighty God, who has knit together thine elect in one communion and fellowship in the mystical body of thy Son Christ our Lord....

> Almighty and everlasting God, who of thy tender love towards mankind has sent thy Son our Saviour Jesus Christ to take upon him our flesh and to suffer death upon the cross, that all mankind should follow the example of his great humility....

> Almighty God, who through thy only begotten Son Jesus Christ hast overcome death and opened unto us the gate of everlasting life....

The Alternative Services Book contains many new collects which powerfully present this same meditative aspect.

> Almighty God, whose most dear Son went not up to joy but first he suffered pain, and entered not into glory before he was crucified....

> God of peace, who brought again from the dead our Lord Jesus Christ, that great shepherd of the sheep, by the blood of the eternal covenant....

Mind and heart are drawn towards Godward reflection before the petitions begin. The more space that is given to this aspect of prayer the more will prayer have the character of listening as well as talking, of converse rather than monologue. While liturgy is indeed meditative it is however in silence that this aspect of prayer has supreme opportunity.

The Bible bears powerful witness to meditative prayer and to the silence which enables it. There are the pleas to men and women to "consider." "Consider the lilies," says Jesus. "Consider this, you that forget God," says the psalmist. In Psalm 8 there is a meditation upon the vastness and wonder of God's creation, and the marvelous role of man within the universe.

For I will consider thy heavens,
    even the works of thy fingers:
the moon and the stars which thou hast ordained.
What is man, that thou art mindful of him;
    and the Son of Man that thou visitest him?
O Lord our governor:
    how excellent is thy name in all the world.
        (Psalm 8:3-4, 10)

The poet is not only describing his belief: he is letting his imagination wonder at it, and he summons his readers to wonder with him. But the power to "consider" is thwarted by the speed in which event follows event, and the noise which events so often involve. So silence has its essential role. In two ways specially the Bible tells of silence in the relation to God. Sometimes the presence or the voice of God reduces men to silence by bringing awe and dread.

Stand in awe, and sin not:
commune with your own heart,
    and in your chamber and be still.
        (Psalm 4:4)

Sometimes men will seek silence in order to listen and hear. Thus Moses and Elijah in turn sought God in the silence of the wilderness. Jesus sought the Father in the stillness of a mountain. Both of those aspects of silence recur in the biblical writings.

Be still then, and know that I am God:
I will be exalted among the heathen,
    and I will be exalted in the earth.
        (Psalm 46:10)

Silence enables us to be aware of God, to let mind and imagination dwell upon his truth, to let prayer be listening before it is talking, and to discover our own selves in a way that is not always possible when we are making or listening to noise. There comes sometimes an interior silence in which the soul discovers itself in a new dimension of energy and peace, a dimension which the restless life can miss. If the possibilities of silence were often hard in biblical times they are infinitely harder in the world in which we live today. A world frightening in its speed and noise is a world where silence alone may enable man's true freedom to be found.

The ways in which meditation interpenetrates the praying of the Church and of the Christian are legion. A time of silence enables the Christian to share more deeply in the Church's sacramental worship. The Eucharist is the Church's central confrontation with the mystery of Christ, who died and rose again. By sharing in the Eucharist the Christian draws strength into his own time of silence, while the time of silence deepens what he brings and gives in the Eucharist. Into the Christian's use of silence there may flow the wonder of God the Creator, the recollection of the life and death and resurrection of Jesus, the recalling of scenes in his life, often a passage of the Bible, the glories of nature in which the finger of God is present, gratitude for personal blessings or the words of poets who tell of wonder and beauty. All these may stir meditation, and its course may be unpredictable.

There is however the discipline of meditation as the deliberate use of a time of silence. Christianity in the West in the last four centuries has owed much, indirectly as well as directly, to the teaching and method of St. Ignatius Loyola, the founder of the Jesuits, in his work *Spiritual Exer-*

cises. These exercises offer a strenuous course of planned meditations, aiming at the conversion of the user into a deeper following of Jesus Christ. The pattern is called the Three-fold Meditation. After prayer for the help of the Holy Spirit and the focusing of the imagination upon the biblical picture or theme there follow the steps described as Memory, Intelligence, and Will. To recall vividly the scene or theme, to think about its meaning, and to offer a resolution drawn from it, that is the way. Imagination, mind and will are all involved. Another method, less formal than the Ignatian, is called the Sulpician, after its use in the parish of St. Sulpice in Paris, through the teaching of J. J. Olier following the guidance of Cardinal de Berulle. In this the pattern is described as Christ before the eyes, Christ in the heart, Christ in the hands. Here indeed is an appealing depth and simplicity. We see Christ in that aspect of him which has been chosen: we drink the message into our heart; we resolve what our response will be. The movement is from eyes to heart and from heart to hands. So may we meditate, and so in other contexts may we pray.

Sometimes concentration breaks down. When it does there may be remedies at hand in a greater discipline and resolution with the help of the Holy Spirit. If however concentration breaks down constantly and it seems irreparable, then it may be a sign that we are being called to pass on to a different way of prayer. What seems to be failure may be the gate to new things in store. In meditation the inability of the eye to concentrate on its seeing, or of the affections to be warmed, or of the mind to be coherent, may mean that the Christian is called to let these faculties rest and to draw out from a deep and often unused part of himself simply a desire for God, however weak that desire may seem to be. Phrases of this kind will be repeated: "My

God I love thee: help me to love thee more," "My God, I believe in thee: increase my faith," "My God, I want thee: help me to want thee more." The repetition of these words many times tells of something deep in you which wants God. Prayer of this kind is sometimes called "the prayer of forced acts." While the acts may at first be those of the affections they soon may become no more than acts of *wanting*, with an awareness that while the wanting is small it is a deep and real part of oneself which longs to be stronger. It is sad that there are many who at this point may abandon prayer feeling it to be a failure, for it may be at this very point that prayer is finding a new nearness to God. It is by its passivity that prayer of this kind opens the way to new pouring of the love and power of God into a soul, which is stripped naked of all but the wanting of God.

When prayer moves thus it is advisable, while still reading the Bible diligently and using the brain in other contexts, to abandon attempts at meditation or brainwork in prayer, and to let prayer become simply a prayer of quiet attention and wanting God. Called sometimes the Prayer of Simplicity, this prayer may be as powerful as it is passive. So far from being remote from the world this kind of prayer may indeed be serving the world as greatly as any prayer by being a channel of God's outflowing love.

We are now on the threshold of the immense theme of Christian Mysticism, a theme which includes some of the greatest of saints and some experiences to which not all Christians are called. But our approach to this theme has been empirical, for there is a contemplation which is near to many Christians and is accessible to all who try to love and serve God and to pray.

The story of mysticism in Christianity passes through the centuries with the names of men and women who prayed and taught others to pray, and some of them wrote books of beauty and wisdom about it. The variety is great, including those who follow a monastic vocation and those who are involved in many practical aspects of the world's life. In some of the mystics a Platonist strain is apparent in their thinking about God, but in others there is no sign of this. Amidst the varieties of culture and historical setting among the mystics an inner unity is apparent. The phenomenon known simply as Contemplation or as Mystical Theology has had certain recurring characteristics.

Two terms, useful but perhaps a little questionable, have sometimes been employed: Infused Contemplation and Acquired Contemplation. The first name describes God's gift to some who have a special vocation to receive it, and the second describes something accessible to all who by the grace of their baptism try to follow the Christian life. But, as any and every prayer and any and every part of Christian life is always of God's gift to us, the phrase "Acquired" is not very happy. But the distinction is rightly made between the contemplation which is accessible to all who are faithful, and the contemplation which is a special gift and vocation. So too the term "a contemplative" can be used in a variety of ways. It is used of those to whom the highest gifts of contemplation are given, and it is used of the wider number of those who are called to have contemplative prayer as their chief work and occupation in life. Neither of these uses of the word should lead us to forget the contemplative prayer which is accessible to all, including those to whom God gives a power of contemplation mingled with a strenuous life of practical service.

Contemplation as the mystics understand it is a prayer in which brain and imagination and the knowledge and enjoyment of God's creatures fade away in a passivity in which the depth of soul is disclosed and the love of God is poured into it. It is the prayer of wanting, receiving and loving. It is always preceded by what is called the Dark Night of the Soul. This phrase does not mean "external" sufferings of mind or body, though the Cross will have its place in the course of any Christian life. Rather does the phrase mean that within the prayer itself there is a darkness, for the reality of God is unlike all one's previous glimpses of him. And the self is stripped of all but the love which God will give and the love which will respond. The darkness is indeed an aspect of God's own light, and the phrase used by one of the mystics—"a ray of darkness"—tells of this. Sometimes the descriptions of the night and of the contemplation are close together like the two sides of one event.

The Dark Night is often described in two phases: the Night of the Senses and the Night of the Spirit. The first of these means the stripping which we have seen to be the prelude to ordinary contemplation. The second precedes the deepest kind of contemplation, and we can only listen to the attempts of experience to describe it. It is the disappearing into darkness of that pattern of faith in God which the soul had believed and known, for such is the mystery of God that when we say that God *is* this or that the reality so transcends the language that it is as true to say God *is not*. If the first of these Nights is the familiar prelude to all contemplation, the second is described by those who have known the deepest contemplation of all.

To try to paraphrase the mystical language is indeed to speak as a fool. Hence one is tempted at this point to give a catena of passages in which the mystics themselves describe what they experienced. But even such a series may fail to convey more than a fraction of the reality, for the mystical experience is not in a vacuum but it is the part of a life offered to the service of God in a way which is also a service of the world. Here however is one glimpse. The anonymous *Cloud of Unknowing,* of which a little more is said in the next chapter, gives as pure an account of contemplation as can be read.

For at the first time when thou dost this work, thou findest but a darkness, and as it were a cloud of unknowing, thou knowest not what, saving that thou feelest in thy will a naked intent unto God. This darkness and this cloud is, however thou dost, between thee and thy God, and telleth thee that thou mayest neither see him clearly by light of understanding nor feel him in sweetness of love in thine affection. Therefore shape thee to abide in this darkness as long as thou mayest, evermore crying after him that thou lovest. For if ever thou shalt feel him or see him, as it may be here, it behoveth always to be in this cloud and in this darkness. Smile upon that thick cloud with a sharp dart of longing love. (Chapter 3)

Then will he sometimes peradventure send out a beam of spiritual light, bursting this cloud of unknowing that is betwixt thee and him; and share thee some of his privity, the which may not speak. Then shalt thou feel thy affection inflamed with the fire of his love, far more than I can tell thee, or may or will at this time. For of that work, that falleth only to God, dare I not take upon me to speak with my blabbering tongue; and shortly to say although I durst I would not. (Chapter 26)

How is contemplation as the mystics have understood it related to Christianity?

There are those who point to a similarity between the contemplation of Christians and the contemplation of Buddhists and people of other faiths. Here indeed the techniques may sometimes be similar. What is different is the context of religion and life in which the contemplation occurs, and for the Christian contemplative that context is of supreme importance. The effect of contemplation is often not to cause the person to long for experiences so much as to love and serve God under the sovereignty revealed in Jesus. Indeed the validity of contemplation is often tested by the pursuit of the life of faith.

There is the problem also of the relation of mysticism in history to Platonist ideas of the divine. There is no doubt that much influence upon the course of Christian mysticism was exercised by the fifth-century Platonist philosophical writer in Syria, who is known sometimes as Dionysius and sometimes as Denys. In his teaching the description of the Night and the contemplative moment is linked with the "Negative Way" which philosophically describes the mystery of God in terms of that which God is *not.* There is however a difference between a Platonism which serves to express some aspects of the Christian revelation of God as utterly mysterious, and a Platonism which can distort it; and it seems fair to say that through the years the Christian mystical tradition has been faithful to the Christian pattern of belief in God as the creator of the world and in Jesus as the divine savior. The difference is between a Platonist idea of the soul of man as inherently divine and so becoming united with deity, and the

Christian belief that the soul of man is a part of the created and now sinful world to be reconciled into seeking union with the creator.

There is also the relation of contemplation to the Christianity of the apostolic age. It is held by some that mysticism involves a ladder of piety up to God in a way that is contrary to the Pauline doctrines of "by faith alone" and "by grace alone." But it seems that the passivity of contemplation is a judgment upon salvation by works and a manifestation of "faith alone" and "grace alone." In different ways both Martin Luther and St. John of the Cross witnessed to the divine judgment upon a Church complacent in tradition and good works and piety. Nowhere in the New Testament writings is there a description of contemplative prayer, unless St. Paul was making a clumsy attempt to refer to it in his mention of one caught up into the third heaven in 2 Corinthians 12. But Christian prayer and Christian life are described both by St. Paul and by St. John as including a deep indwelling of God and of Jesus in the Christians, an anticipation of the glory of the parousia. We are not far from contemplation when we read, "If a man love me he will keep my word, and my Father will love him and we will come and make our dwelling with him."

Chapter 9

The Way of the Mystics

T he saints and the classics of Christian mysticism are spread through many lands and centuries. Since we turn to other epochs and other lands for inspiration in different forms of sanctity, to a St. Francis in medieval Italy, or to the martyrs in Uganda in the modern world, so we learn from the saints of mysticism without the distinction of time and place. In this chapter we shall look at two groups of mystics who sometimes catch the imagination of Christians today by speaking to our own souls. These groups are the English mystics of the fourteenth century and the Carmelites of sixteenth-century Spain. Their inner unity with one another is striking and so is their voice to us.

At the time when much of England was desolated by the Black Death there appeared some Christian writers who described in beautiful English the Godward journey of prayer, with teaching drawn from their own deep experience. They wrote with both a monastic background of prayer and learning and the kind of setting characteristic of the hermit whose spiritual help is sought by many people. Here indeed was spirituality for the people.

There was a Yorkshireman, Richard Rolle of Hampole, and after his death in 1349 his writings were collected by the Cistercian nuns whose spiritual adviser he had been. He wrote many poems and meditations, his most famous work being *The Fire of Love*. Here he described the joy of prayer in its many phases, with union with God as the goal, and he did so with warmth and fervor. The prayer which he describes is not precisely that of passive contemplation for it is filled with feeling and some might describe it as "charismatic." But prayer for him is always by the way of the Cross.

> Either in this life the fire of divine wrath will consume the rest of our sins and give charity to our souls....Or after this life the fire of purgatory will pain our souls....O good Jesus scourge me here, pierce me here, strike me here, burn me here, that in the future I have no evil but may feel thy love here and for ever.

Amidst the fervor of a love of God and love of people he is in no doubt that contemplation is the goal.

The Cloud of Unknowing comes from an unknown writer with a deep knowledge of mystical tradition and a terse English style of simplicity. It is as pure and classical an account of contemplation as can be found, with uncompromising emphasis upon the Dark Night and the passive reception of the divine love. Mysticism and theology find exposition in a winning English way.

> To the knowing power God is evermore incomprehensible, but to the loving power he is, in every man diversely, all comprehensible to the full....For why, love may reach to God in this life, but not knowing....And therefore she [Mary Magdalene] hung up

her love in this cloud of unknowing and learned to
love a thing the which she might not see clearly in
this life by lot of understanding in her reason.
(Chapter 46)

The writer would warn the readers about the kind of
"sweetness" which Rolle expounded. She says, "All other
efforts, sounds and quietness and sweetness that comes
from without I pray thee have them suspect. All sweetness
and comforts, bodily or ghostly, be to those as it were acci-
dents...lean not too much on them...when peradventure
thou mayest be stirred to love God for the sake of him."
Concerning the goal there come these aspiring words, "For
not what thou art, nor what thou hast been, shall God see
with his merciful eyes, but what thou wouldest be" (Chapter 132).

Walter Hilton, doctor of Paris and monk at Throgmorton
in Northamptonshire (died 1396), was a teacher rather different from these. He wrote as one who sought the goal in
its night and glory, but he did so as a pastor eager to stand
at the very bottom and to guide us step by step. His theme
was the whole Christian life, and all the steps are traced in
his work appropriately called *The Ladder of Perfection*. He
is sure that the heights of prayer are available by the grace
of God that is given to every baptized Christian. He is very
gentle. No writer expounds the approach to the Night of
the Senses with more gentle sympathy for the frightened.
But most striking is the evangelical fervor with which he
tells of the person of Jesus as himself the guide and the
way. It is Jesus, who "formeth and reformeth," therefore
"dread not, for the fire will not hurt thee." It is Jesus who
gives us our good desires and shares them as making
them his own.

God openeth the eyes of the soul and showeth to the
soul the sight of Jesus wonderfully, and the knowing
of him, as the soul may suffer it thus by little and by
little; and by that sight he raiseth all the affections of
the soul to him.... This love is nought else but Jesus
himself, who for love worketh all this in a man's soul
and reformeth it in feeling to his likeness.

With this intense devotion to Jesus the writer is also so
mindful of the Father and the Spirit that he dwells upon
Christian prayer as our relation to the blessed Trinity.

Is a Christianity with such emphasis on contemplative
prayer able to speak widely to men and women of many
kinds with practical power? The answer is seen near at
hand in the Lady Julian of Norwich. She was a mystic and
her writing alludes to her experience of contemplation not
least in accounts of the finding of God as linked with the
finding of one's own self. But her *Revelations of Divine
Love is* significant not as an exposition of contemplation,
about which it does not say a great deal, but as showing
what a Christian mystic can give to the world as poet, vi-
sionary, pastor, prophet, theologian. From the root there
comes the marvelous fruit. Julian has been much read and
much described in recent years: in this chapter my concern is with how her mysticism relates to the other aspects
of Christianity.

On 8 May 1375 she saw the visions. It was twenty-one
years later that she wrote her account of them, with her
deep reflections and interpretations of their meaning. Visions of Jesus, interpreted by the mind and heart of a poet
and theologian, that is Julian, and the reflections stretch
over a whole range of Christian faith and life. The Passion
of Jesus is the source of the revelations and the key to the
questions which arise.

So the theme begins with the longing in her heart. It was a longing for a bodily sight of the Passion, for true contrition and for three wounds: "the wound of very contrition, the wound of kind compassion, and the wound of steadfast longing toward God." The three wounds pervade the visions and the reflections. Thus the vision of the Trinity as the perfection of love flows from her sight of the Passion:

> In this moment suddenly I saw the red blood trickle down from under the garland hot and freshly and right plenteously, as it were in the time of his Passion when the garland of thorns was pressed on his blessed head who was both God and Man, the same that suffered thus for me. I can see truly and madly that it was himself showed it to me without any mean. And in the same showing suddenly the Trinity fulfilled my heart most of joy. And so I understood it shall be in heaven without end to all that shall come there. For the Trinity is God. The Trinity is our maker and keeper, the Trinity is our everlasting love and everlasting joy and peace by our Lord Jesus Christ, and this was showed in the first showing and in awe. For where Jesus appears the blessed Trinity is understood as to my sight. (Chapter 4)

So too the love in the Passion is the key to the vision of the creator's love for his creatures. This is not always remembered by those who specially love Julian's vision of the created world.

> Also in this he showed me a little thing, the quantity of a hazel nut, in the palm of my hand; and it was round as a ball. I looked thereon with the eye of my understanding, and thought: What might this be?

And it was answered generally thus: It is all that is made. I marvelled how it might last, for methought it might suddenly have fallen to nought for littleness. And I was answered in my understanding: It lasteth and ever shall last for that God loveth it. And so all the thing hath being by the love of God. (Chapter 5)

So the theme proceeds with marvelous variety and inner unity, for it is the blood of Jesus which reveals the kind compassion of our creator Lord. Very striking is the language about Divine Motherhood, an image which describes not the creator's care for the world but the redeeming work of Jesus which is seen as the motherly bringing to birth of those who belong to the new creation. So far from causing thought and questioning to be overwhelmed the movement of the work stirs Julian to hard thinking, not least about the problem of evil in the world. Two attempts at an intellectual answer break down, before she frames the act of faith, only in the context of the Passion, "All shall be well, and all shall be well and all manner of things shall be well."

Here is just a glimpse of the poetry and theology and prophecy coming from one who has known the depth of contemplation in its discovery of the love of God and the ground of her own soul. The visions, the ecstasies, the poetry, the reflections, are not contemplation, but they are its fruits in the outpouring of the love of God.

Wouldest thou learn thy Lord's meaning in this thing? Learn it well: Love is its meaning. Who showed it thee? Love. What showed it thee? Love. Hold thee therein and thou shalt learn and know more in the same, but if thou shalt never know nor learn therein every thing without end. Thus was it I learned that Love was our Lord's meaning. (Chapter 86)

✝

If suffering is often the soil in which sanctity grows this is the background of the lives of St. Teresa and St. John of the Cross. Monasticism in Spain in the sixteenth century had become worldly and complacent. Within the Carmelite Order there was a growing movement of reform called the Discalced Carmelites, devoted to the revival of the primitive rule and to prayer, fellowship and simplicity. But the dominant part of the Order would have none of this, and those seeking the reform were subjected to persecution and cruelty. That was the context in which Teresa and John were plunged. Teresa, born in 1515, entered the Carmelite Monastery of the Incarnation at Avila in 1552 and she drew other Carmelites after her in her zeal for reform and spirituality, founding in 1572 the Convent of St. Joseph. The inner life made known in her writings was one with a life of strenuous activity in traveling on foot, teaching, organizing, and giving pastoral care to many people older and younger. Contemplation and action were both hers in full and mingled measure.

Teresa's writings are vivid in poetic images of many kinds and in the accounts of her visions and ecstasies. She can describe the spiritual life as the watering of a garden, as a game of chess, as the story of a silkworm, as a journey through the rooms of a castle, as the tossing of a ship on the waves. She writes as a teacher and guide, and more than many contemplative writers she tells of the anticipations of the heights which appear in the early stages of the climb. These characteristics appear in each of her three great works, *The Life, The Way of Perfection,* and *The Interior Castle.*

The Life tells of visions and ecstasies which have helped Teresa on her way: visions of Jesus and visions of hell which in early years led her to her decision. She describes in this work the early stages of prayer accessible to all Christians, and beginners are again and again in her care. Here comes the watering of the garden as an image of the stages of prayer. There must first be the drastic weeding of the soil. Then the stages in the art of watering correspond to the struggle for prayer to become less our own doing and more God's action within us. First, there is the stage in which we carry water from a well, the stage of laborious effort in meditation. Then there is the stage in which the use of a windlass is found, with the discovery that prayer is far more the work of God himself than we had realized. Then there is the stage when a brook flows on to the ground and wonderfully softens it. Finally we realize that the best thing of all is drenching rain, the divine love being poured into the soul: "By heavy rain when the Lord waters it with no labour of ours, a way in comparison better than any of those which have been described" *(The Life,* Chapters 14-16).

Images as vivid as these abound in *The Life,* and they tell us both about the Christian way and about Teresa, whose ceaseless activity was mingled with the Prayer of Quiet as she describes it. This is a prayer not to be confused with the goal of contemplation, but one which is accessible to all who are faithful in prayer and humility. She kept the word "contemplation" for the deep passive experience which is the goal. But she knew prayer which anticipates the goal: "our strife can be borne if we find peace where we live." "O, if only I could tell you of the quiet and calm in which my soul finds itself. For it is now so certain that it will have the goal of heaven and it seems to be in possession of it already."

The Way of Perfection is a more concentrated work telling of the following of Christ in the life of fellowship and humility in the community for which Teresa is writing. Indeed, while much teaching on prayer is given there is little dwelling on prayer as a thing in itself, for prayer and life are of one piece in the soul's relation to God. While contemplation is the goal, not all are called now to be contemplatives. Many callings are embraced within the community: "Remember there must be someone to cook the meals, and count yourselves happy to be able to serve like Martha" (Chapter 17). Nor is there a rigid line between vocal and mental prayer, for vocal prayer which attends carefully to God becomes meditative and may not be far from the Prayer of Quiet. But the gentleness of Teresa's counsels never becomes softness, as a passage like this shows: "I want you, my daughters, to be strong men. If you do all that is in you the Lord will make you so manly that men themselves will be amazed at you."

The Interior Castle is more rambling in style and this may be due to the years of strain in which Teresa found herself, with the controversies and the strenuous travelling on foot visiting the Carmelite houses and building them up amidst ceaseless difficulty. The theme is now the progress of the soul into Contemplation. The imagery is a journey from the outer court of a castle into its inner chamber, and the journey is both into the life of God and into the depth of the soul. The journey is not easy, for, as we open the first door by which we enter, horrible snakes and reptiles from the courtyard want to get in with us to our continuing discomfort. The series of mansions is thus described. The first is Humility. The second is Prayer. The third is Meditation and Exemplary Life. The fourth is the Prayer of Quiet. The fifth is the Spiritual Betrothal. The sixth is the Night of the Spirit. The seventh is the Spiritual Marriage.

It will be seen that the first four mansions belong to the Christian life as much practiced and as taught in Teresa's earlier writings. It is when we approach the last three mansions that the distinctively contemplative vocation comes into its own. The Betrothal is a union with God, deep and joyful, which lasts a short while, indeed but half an hour, and it is the sure anticipation of what will come after. The soul at this stage "cannot possibly doubt that it has been in God and God has been in it." Meanwhile Night follows; and it is described as other contemplatives describe it, and its pains are "the wounds of love."

But Teresa cannot tell of the final stages of Night and Spiritual Marriage without recourse to other images besides the journey through the Castle. So there is the image of the silkworm; burying itself in the cocoon it dies to self and out comes the lovely butterfly. So also the image of water is used: first, there is the ship tossed upon the waves, then there is the river that flows into the sea merging itself totally with the ocean. This image would suggest indeed the disappearance of the soul's identity in God, were it not that other images and teachings show that the soul finds its own self in God.

Teresa died in 1582 on the Feast of St. Francis. No Christian can have borne witness to the blending of contemplative prayer and vigorous and painful activity more powerfully than she did. Ten years before her death she had experienced the union with God described as Spiritual Marriage, and it is hard to doubt that this goal and her ceaseless quest for it were the secret of her powerful influence in prayer, humility, and compassion.

St. John of the Cross (1542-91) assisted Teresa in the care and defence of the Reformed Carmelites, but he differed from her in his training and experience and in the emphasis of his teaching. He brought from the University of Salamanca a store of learning in the traditions of mysticism, and a mind more clear and concentrated. His sufferings were terrible, and his life was indeed marked by the Cross, with which his name has been linked for all time.

Devoting himself to the reform of the Carmelites and after holding several offices in that Order, he was kidnapped by the unreformed authorities and imprisoned in a cell in a monastic house in Toledo. Nine months he spent in the cell only four feet by six in size. There was no outside window, and to get light to read his breviary he had to stand on a stool near a hole through which light came from an adjacent room. His meals were taken on the floor of the refectory, and after them he was scourged on his bare shoulders. The trauma ended after nine months when he made an adventurous escape on 16 August 1578; but this was not before he had with a little paper and ink available written in the cell a good deal of his lovely poem *The Spiritual Canticle.*

We who do not read Spanish can get only a glimpse of the loveliness of this work in the English translations. It is written in the idiom of the Song of Solomon, with a dialogue between the bridegroom and the bride, sublimated into the longing for heaven and the beauty and peace of God. This work was followed by *The Ascent of Mount Carmel,* a work in part poetical and in part a prose commentary upon the stanzas. There followed *The Dark Night of the Soul,* expounding the classical mystical teaching with a good deal of the kind of thought which had appeared in *The Cloud of Unknowing* in England two centuries earlier. The distinctiveness of St. John of the Cross is seen in the contrast with St. Teresa. Unlike her he made no appeal to visions and ecstasies as an authority. Indeed he was very critical of the claims for visions and ecstasies in the Christian life. Unlike her he did not write for a Christian community in its various stages or aspects: he wrote for those with a definite contemplative vocation to guide them in their path. Nor did he have an autobiographical note in his teaching, for while his sufferings attuned him to the way of the Cross and to the acceptance of the Dark Night, he was very clear that the Dark Night is derived from the true nature of prayer itself as it approaches the contemplation of God. The Night has a large place in his teaching, for whereas Teresa held that a kind of contemplation called the Prayer of Quiet is possible within Christian life before ever the Night comes, St. John allows nothing of a contemplative kind and no authentic quietness until first there has been the Night of the Senses.

St. John himself is sometimes frightening. At the beginning of the *Ascent* he says:

> The journey of the soul to the divine union is called night for three reasons: the point of departure is privation of all desire, and complete detachment from the world; the road is by faith, which is like night to the intellect; the goal which is God is incomprehensible while we are in this life....Empty thy spirit of all created things, and thou wilt walk in the divine light, for God resembles no created thing.

But beyond the night is God himself;

His sweetest love of God but little known; he who has found thee is at rest; let everything be changed, O God, that we may rest in thee. Everything with thee, O my God, every way all things with thee; as I see, O my love, all for thee, nothing for me—nothing for me, everything for thee....I will draw near to thee in silence and will uncover thy feet, that it may please thee to unite me to thyself making my soul thy bride; I will rejoice in nothing till I am in thine arms. O Lord I beseech thee, leave me not for a moment, because I know not the worth of my own soul.

It is important in reading St. Teresa and St. John of the Cross to be sure to whom they are writing and about what. St. Teresa is often writing about the many phases of Christian life within her community with varieties of vocation, though always with contemplation as the goal. St. John is more often writing of the contemplative vocation through the Night. His words about self-negation and indeed self-destruction are sometimes grim and frightening, but the Night is not an act of the self so much as the first part of the divine gift leading to light and glory and reflected in the service of man. The act of self-surrender is called for, and here St. John seems very near to the words of Jesus about losing life so as to find it, and near also to the words of St. Paul about counting all his good things to be dung as compared with the following of the crucified.

Be still and know. These two groups of mystics whom we have been considering, English and Spanish, illustrate the contemplative vocation through the centuries and its power to speak to our own times as to any other. It is too early to assess the place in the history of mysticism of one who belongs to our own time, such as Thomas Merton, but it is clear that his radical abandonment of the world in his contemplative vocation brought him nearer to the world's heart.

> The monk searches not only his own heart: he plunges deep into the heart of that world of which he remains a part although he seems to have left it. In reality he abandons the world only in order to listen more intently to the voices that proceed from its inmost depths.
>
> (*The Climate of Monastic Prayer*, p. 35)

It matters greatly for the renewal of the Christian Church that the contemplative vocation be more known and recovered. It matters for us all, whatever our own form of service, for we are all one family. Just as it helps us in our day-to-day struggles that there are martyrs who have given their lives for Christ, so it helps us in our feeble praying that there are those who know the Dark Night and have God himself poured into their souls. We are all one family and we share one life in Christ.

Chapter 10

Confessing Our Sins

The climax of the Eucharist is the showing forth of the Lord's death and our reception of Jesus crucified and risen to be our food. It is a climax of mingled awe and intimacy. Earlier in the service there has been another crucial event whose momentous character is not always realized. It is when we confess that we have been sinners and hear the word of God's absolution proclaimed by the celebrant. Familiarity may blur the immense issues which are at stake, for our sins concern the crucifixion of Jesus and so does the giving of God's forgiveness.

The older Anglican rites place the confession and absolution some distance within the service after the Prayer of Intercession, but the newer Anglican rites allow the confession and absolution to come at the very beginning of the service; and this gives greater prominence to the confession of our sins as a preparation for all that follows and at a time when attention may be more likely. But in either case, how often is it that the congregation saying the confession are remembering what their sins have actually been, having prepared themselves for this before, and how often is it realized that the absolution is the momentous act of God's own forgiveness?

The forgiveness of God is costly. It does not mean a declaration that sin does not matter so very much: rather is it an act which affirms the divine hatred of sin and invites us to share in that hatred at the moment when God's compassion flows to us. Calvary tells of the cost of God's forgiveness and of the character of our sin as a selfishness and pride which wounds our relation to God. By the depth of their realization of what penitence and forgiveness mean, Christian people are helping a deeper holiness in the life of the Church.

Experience shows that it is necessary before we come to the liturgy to settle in our hearts the relation of our sins to the divine pardon. Indeed the exhortations in Cranmer's Prayer Book urge that the issue be faced before we come to the service and before the confession and absolution in the service happen.

Our Anglican Church allows us a wise liberty. We are free to confess our sins in our prayer to God, sure that if our confession has been careful and complete the forgiveness of God comes to us. There is no doubt of that. We are also free, if we are so drawn, to confess our sins in the presence of the priest who will give us sacramental absolution in the name and by the authority of Jesus Christ. Those who freely choose this latter way do so because it is thorough and rather painful, and they feel that both thoroughness and pain are not amiss; and there is also the joyful decisiveness of the sacramental absolution. So far from being the intrusion of a priest between the soul and God, the absolution makes vivid the decisiveness of divine forgiveness in word and act.

Repentance, *metanoia*, is the turning of the mind, and with the mind the imagination, the affections and the will, away from self and sin and towards God. It is within an act of Godward-turning that our self-examination happens. We look towards God in gratitude for his loving-kindness, towards Jesus in his death for our sins, towards our own true self in what it is meant to become. The examining of our consciences will be thorough, and while it means a looking into ourselves it will not be an introspective self-scrutiny, for it will be mingled with the looking up towards God and the exposing of the self towards him. But the preparation will be thorough. It is not a matter of naming those sins which seem to be "big" or which worry us specially, for it is necessary to confess all the ways in which our attitudes and actions have been contrary to the Christian way. That is important. It is a confession of the whole self, and the attitudes and actions which we may sometimes think to be small may be a decisive part of the self's orientation.

Preparation for the sacrament, however, is not only the preparing of a list of our sins. It is also a preparation for the grace of absolution and the presence of Jesus the absolver. The absolution is a real confrontation with the Lord Jesus, who died for us and now lives. And we prepare to meet him in his holiness and his compassion. It makes a world of difference if this aspect is given prominence in the preparation, and sacramental confession can be a meeting with Jesus as wonderful and decisive as meeting him in Holy Communion.

There has sadly been a decline in the use of confession. Whereas earlier in the century the use of confession had grown widely in many parts of the Anglican Church irrespective of partisan considerations, a decline has undoubtedly occurred in the last two decades. A number of causes have been at work. In part the decline is due to confusion about right and wrong and the nature of authority. In part it is due to the availability of many new kinds of counseling for people with troubles and problems, particularly counseling of a psychological kind. But the chief cause has without doubt been the weakening of the sense of sin and the paramount issues of God, sin, and holiness. It is one thing to learn to "accept one's own humanity," but it is another thing to repent of our misuse of it before God. It is one thing to be freed from the compulsion of unconscious complexes, it is another thing to use that freedom for God's glory.

The renewal of penitence in the Church involves, however, not only a revival of well-attested practice, but a looking for new ways in the expression of that practice and a new vision of the immense issues of reconciliation.

New developments in the form of confession and absolution have appeared both in the Roman Catholic Church and in the Anglican Communion in recent years. In the Roman Catholic Church a desire for a rite less formal and less individualistic, while being still deeply sacramental, led to the publication of a new *Ordo Poenitentiae* in December 1973. This *Ordo* provides both a new form for private confession and absolution, and a new corporate rite of penitence. The former includes a dialogue of prayer and counsel between priest and penitent in a context rather wider than the specific sins which are confessed, while the sacramental absolution remains the climax. The latter provides a ministry of the Word leading to a corporate act of penitence in a congregation, followed in turn by private confessions to the priests, and ending with a corporate thanksgiving by all. Within the Anglican Communion the American Church has a new rite for the Reconciliation of a

Penitent, somewhat similar to the new Roman Order. These reforms are as yet in an experimental stage, and they are sometimes found to have a fussy self-consciousness. As experiments develop it will be important that they do not lose the sacramental simplicity which has brought great strength in the past.

Renewal in the ministry of reconciliation, however, goes deeper and wider than the style of rite. The ministry of reconciliation is part of the life of a reconciled and reconciling Church. This means a Church aware that it owes its own existence to the reconciliation of the Cross, and has a worship ever deepened by that awareness. It means also a Church which prays for the world with the question "Who is my neighbor?" ceaselessly in heart and mind and outgoing action. Within the reconciling prayer and action is the Christian concern about relations with people of other races, about poverty and hunger in the world, about cruelty and injustice, and about weapons of destruction. Within our confession of our sins there will come sins of attitude or complacency or idleness of thought. We are not sinning if we are unsure of the answers to hard questions. We are sinning if we do not think or care. All this is part of a renewed ministry of reconciliation.

Distinct from the ministry of absolution is the ministry of spiritual direction, although the two are often linked. In confession the penitent asks for "penance, counsel and absolution" and the counseling given in that context may be full of wisdom and encouragement. Many owe to it more than they can say. But spiritual direction may be given quite apart from confession, and its context is not only the tale of sins but the pattern of a person's life with its opportunities and frustrations. Needless to say, the term direction does not mean the giving of orders, but advice about the spiritual journey from one who, perhaps ahead of us, knows something of the pitfalls, the mists and the bogs, as well as the lovely vistas, not least in the life of prayer. "Counseling" has often come to mean advice of a psychological kind directed to wholeness, and the training for it is, alas, all too often neglectful of the art of helping people in the life of prayer and as neglectful of the treasures of Christian spirituality.

Chapter 11

The Communion
of Saints

The prayer of a Christian is prayer with all the saints, and the phrase "Communion of Saints" tells of this. These words have both a richness and a simplicity which are often missed, for the original Latin *communio sanctorum* could mean both the fellowship of holy people and the participation in holy things, especially the sacred elements in the Eucharist. The phrase began to appear in Western baptismal creeds only from the fifth century, being inserted between "the Holy Catholic Church" and "the forgiveness of sins." Whether the original reference was to the sacraments or to the fellowship of saints has been much debated, but the latter interpretation came to prevail widely. The two understandings indeed interpenetrate, for when Christians share in the body and blood of Christ they so share as members of one another.

Hagios, sanctus, holy. God alone is holy, transcendent, beyond all that is creaturely, finite, passing, tainted or blemished. When the Holy God invades a place or a scene, a building or a person, men and women are over-whelmed in awe and bewilderment. But God may indeed make himself present in things, like the sacramental gifts, and God may no less be present in persons who are made *sancti, hagioi,* and all Christians are thus described by the New Testament writers. While Israel had been God's holy people separated from the world to worship him and learn his righteousness, holiness in the New Testament teaching belongs now to the Christians in a deeper personal inti-macy. Every Christian is called to be a saint, and all Chris-tians are described as the saints. The Holy Spirit makes them holy from their union with the risen life of Jesus. They are themselves the temple of God's presence.

The other word *koinonia, communio,* means participa-tion, and according to the New Testament writers the be-lievers participate in the Father and in the Son, they participate in the Spirit, they participate in the body and blood of Christ, in the sufferings of Christ, and in the lives of one another. Inevitably therefore the theme of holiness and the theme of participation interpenetrate, for the Holy Spirit in making the believers holy lifts them out of their isolation so that to share in the Spirit is to share in one an-other. The phrase which we translate "the fellowship of the Holy Spirit" tells of this twofold participation.

Does the participation of Christians in Christ and with one another end at death? If Christianity had done no more than continue some of the older patterns of Jewish belief, that might be so. But into those patterns there now comes the new transforming factor of life with Christ and in Christ, and death does not destroy that. In St. Paul's teaching about the last things the dead are called "the dead in Christ" (1 Thessalonians 4:16), and again "those who are Christ's" (1 Corinthians 15:23). Later St. Paul, already possessing life with Christ and in Christ, refers to his possible death as a departure to "be with Christ, which is far better" (Philippians 1:23). Jesus, according to St. Luke, tells the dying thief on Good Friday that he will that very day be with Christ in Paradise. The life with Christ invades existing patterns of belief with the promise of its continuance after death. We have seen already how the Epistle to the Hebrews describes the Christians as having already come to the heavenly Jerusalem, innumerable hosts of angels and the spirits of just men made perfect (Hebrews 12:22-23).

It is not to be inferred that for those who have died, the life with Christ is immediately a state of perfection and enjoyment of the beatific vision. Indeed Christian tradition both in the East and in the West has assumed that those who have died in faith need cleansing and sanctifying towards the perfect union with God and the vision of him. This state of waiting and cleansing has sometimes been called purgatory, sometimes the intermediate state, sometimes only by the lovely word "Paradise."

Not surprisingly, the belief in the Communion of Saints through the centuries became exposed to speculative and superstitious developments, and we need not here trace how in the Middle Ages in the West the concept of purgatory became corrupted by commercial and legalistic ideas, and how the cult of the saints grew into treating them virtually as mediators. There followed violent reactions in Reformation times leading to a shrinking from prayer for the departed and from any veneration of the saints. In the Anglican Communion and elsewhere there has been a steady recovery of the more primitive concepts, with prayer for the departed and the commemoration of the saints finding its place within the Church's worship, but deep renewal is needed if the Communion of Saints is to be realized in ancient meaning and power.

In this renewal it has been salutary to turn to the Eastern Orthodox Church which has a powerful tradition of fellowship between the Church on earth and the Church in Paradise and in heaven, and then to turn once more to the basic concepts of holiness and participation.

When the Western Christian experiences the worship of the Eastern Orthodox Church he is likely to feel how vivid is the sense of the union of earth and heaven. In the liturgy the Church on earth, through the presence of the Risen Jesus, is sharing already in the worship of heaven with the saints and the angels. Words of St. John Chrysostom tell of this:

> When thou seest the Lord sacrificed and lying as an oblation, and the priest standing by and praying, dost thou think that thou art still among men, and still standing on earth? Nay, thou art translated to heaven, so as to cast out every carnal thought and with unimpeded soul and clean mind to behold the things that are in heaven. *(On the Priesthood, 3, 4)*

Within the liturgy the saints pray for one another and ask for one another's prayers, and the saints include the glorious ones who reflect the glory of Christ and those who are far from perfect, whether they are beyond death or struggling sinners on earth. All pray for all.

> All of us who partake of the one bread and the one cup do thou unite to one another in the communion of one Holy Spirit, and grant that no one of all of us may partake of that holy body and blood unto judgement and unto condemnation, but that we may find mercy and grace together with all thy saints who in

all ages have been acceptable unto thee. For the repose and remission of sins of thy servants, give them rest, O God, in a place where sorrow and sighing have fled away. Give them rest where the light of thy countenance shall visit them, especially our most holy and undefiled and most blessed and glorious Lady, the birth-giver of God and ever-Virgin Mary; and John the Prophet, forerunner and baptist, the holy and glorious apostles, the saint whose memory we now commemorate, and all thy saints, through whose prayers do thou visit us, O God. And call to remembrance all those who have fallen asleep before us in the hope of resurrection unto life eternal. Give them rest where the light of thy countenance shall visit them.

Within this liturgical prayer there are some deep convictions.

1. First, while the claims of sanctity are uncompromising, for God is holy, there is no rigid frontier between saints in glory, saints who are being cleansed in Paradise and saints now struggling with their sins. To Western ideas, where praying *for* the departed and praying *to* the saints are somewhat separate, this Eastern language is striking. In the family of Jesus all pray for all and all ask for the prayers of all amidst the unique glory of Jesus.

2. Within this tradition the holiness of God is related both to persons and to things, and both material things and persons may reflect God's holiness in graciousness and in awe and dread. Thus the icons are venerated and they are both symbols of the saints whom they depict and symbols of God's presence in his sacramental world.

3. The role of Mary is apparent. Her role has been a great one in the bringing of the Communion of Saints into

existence, for it was by divine grace and human response, divine command and human obedience, that the Incarnation happened and God's new creation was begun. As God-bearer, Mary has helped in the creation of the Communion of Saints. As creature with ourselves she gives glory to her creator and ours, to her savior and ours. Herself more glorious than the cherubim and higher than the seraphim she leads our praises to God.

To glance thus at the Christian East and to witness its worship is to have now vision of the Communion of Saints. Concerning Anglican teaching, let one significant Anglican divine be mentioned, Bishop John Pearson of Chester whose work *The Exposition of the Creed* was published in 1669. Pearson recaptures the early concept of participation, showing how the saints on earth participate in the Father, in the Son, in the Holy Spirit, in the angels and in those saints who are now in heaven. No less do they participate with those Christians who are far from saintly and indeed somewhat nominal through their sins and imperfections. "I am fully persuaded," he says,

> as of a necessary and infallible truth, that such persons as are truly sanctified while they live among the crooked generations of men and struggle with the miseries of this world, have fellowship with God the Father, God the Son, and God the Holy Ghost, as belonging with them and taking up their habitation with them; and with them they partake of the care and kindness of the blessed angels who take delight in ministration for their benefit...and they have a communion and conjunction with all the saints on earth as the living members of Christ. Nor is this communion separated by the death of any, but as Christ is he in whom they live from the foundation of

the world, so for them fellowship is with all the saints which from the death of Abel have departed in the faith and power of God and now enjoy the presence of the Father and follow the Lamb whithersoever he goeth. Thus I believe the Communion of Saints." (Article 9)

Elsewhere Bishop Pearson writes movingly about the Blessed Virgin Mary.

It was her own prediction, "from henceforth all generations shall call me blessed"; but the obligation is ours, so to call her, so to esteem her. If Elizabeth cried out with so loud a voice, "Blessed art thou among women," when Christ was but newly conceived in her womb, what expression of honour and admiration could we think sufficient, now that Christ is in heaven and with her. Far be it from any Christian to derogate from that special privilege granted to her which is incommunicable to any other. We cannot forbear to reverence the Mother of our Lord, so long as we give her not that worship which is due unto the Lord himself. Let us keep the language of the primitive Church, let her be honoured and esteemed, let him be worshipped and adored. (Article 2)

Within those writers and documents there is a recapturing of the true concepts of holiness and participation, and it is in these concepts that the understanding of the Communion of Saints is to be sought. Our deeper realization of the Communion of Saints turns however not only upon our understanding of the saints but upon our understanding of the nature of prayer. If our prayer is shaped by our own needs and requests then we may slip into thinking of the saints as those who answer our prayers by dispensing favors to us. If however our prayer is shaped by the giving of glory to God in the quest of his will and his Kingdom, then we may be lifted out of ourselves in the company of those who in Paradise and heaven seek that glory and reflect it. Some words from Richard Meux Benson's *Spiritual Letters* are worth quoting.

> We do not desire to get something by asking for the intercession of a saint, as I fear people very often do desire and seek that intercession accordingly. Our communion with departed saints is of a much deeper character. It is the expression of our united delight in giving glory to Jesus.

It is thus within the reflection of Christ's glory that the prayers of all the saints continue. Within the family of the saints we may ask the prayers of those who are near to the vision of God, and we may pray for all in earth or Paradise or heaven. But we do not forget that the family includes those who are weak and struggling like ourselves, and those whose saintliness is very faint because the world has been reclaiming them. Our prayer looks towards the weak as well as towards the strong, and if we are faithful it will reach both ways since the glory of Christ is always one with the agony of his compassion. Such is the meaning of "I believe in the Communion of Saints."

Chapter 12

Epilogue

C hristian prayer and Christian life are properly inseparable. As the Sonship of Jesus on earth was a relation to the Father in words, in wordless converse and in the obedience of a life and death, so the adopted sonship of the Christians has its facets of word and silence and act. The Sonship of Jesus was to the Father's glory, and in the serving of that glory he consecrated himself on the world's behalf. So too the Christians know the worship of God to be first of all, and know also that this worship is an idolatrous perversion unless it is reflected in compassion towards the world. "As the soul is in the body so are the Christians in the world."

Within the worship of the Christians are acts of wonder at the beauty of God in the created world and his transcending holiness beyond it; and acts of gratitude for his costly redemption of mankind in Jesus. It is a worship in which sometimes the mind and the imagination dwell upon God's beauty and goodness, and sometimes mind and imagination enter the darkness as the unimaginable love of God is poured into the soul. It is a worship whereby the pain of the world is held upon the heart in God's presence, and the desires of men are turned towards the desire of God as we pray in the name of Jesus.

This book has recalled some of the phases in a continuing story. There is the inarticulate yearning towards God found in the human race before and behind the more conscious yearning of the world's religions. There is Israel's worship of its King and Father who is also the world's creator. There is the *Abba* prayer of Jesus in life and in death, and his teaching of the disciples to "pray like this," to utter their desires and frame them to the divine will. There is the fuller revelation of the Father in the death and resurrection of Jesus, evoking the prayer of St. Paul and many others. There is the summary through the veil in the Epistle to the Hebrews with an otherworldliness which gives reality to the present life. There are the mount and the plain which are the scenes of the Lord's exodus. Through the centuries the story continues.

It has been the Christian conviction that the goal of heaven is anticipated in the present life. The Holy Spirit is the first fruits of the heavenly harvest, the first installment of the heavenly treasure, and the Christians in the apostolic age believed their life in Christ to be an anticipation of the goal which was to come. Both the life in Christ in St. Paul and the eternal life here and now in St. John tell of this. Indeed the words "your life is hid with Christ in God" suggest that heaven is not only the goal towards which we journey but a treasure locked in our hearts and one day to be made visible to our eyes (Colossians 3:1-2).

Here the Christian Eucharist speaks. In the Eucharist, with the Risen Jesus present as our food, we are worshiping with the saints and the angels in heaven. But the Risen Jesus who is the heart of the heavenly worship is also a Jesus who was crucified, and we share in heaven's worship only as sharing also in the Jesus who suffers in the world around us, reminding us to meet him there and to serve him in those who suffer. Indeed in the Eucharist we are summoned by two voices, which are really one voice: "Come, the heavenly banquet is here. Join with me and my mother and my friends in the heavenly supper." "Come, I am here in this world in those who suffer. Come to me, come with me, and serve me in them."

But how may we think of heaven? Christianity has known many pictures of heaven from the Apocalypse of John onwards. But here let some words of St. Augustine be recalled, for they are words which not only tell of heaven but are also powerfully suggestive of heaven's present anticipations. In his work *The City of God* St. Augustine told of heaven thus.

> We shall rest and we shall see, we shall see and we shall love, we shall love and we shall praise, in the end which is no end.

Rest: we shall be freed from the busy and fussy activity in which we get in our own light and expose ourselves to our self-centeredness. Resting, we shall find that we **see** in a new way, without the old hindrances. We shall see our neighbors as what they really are, creatures and children of God in whom is the divine image, and that image will become newly visible to us. We shall see ourselves too as God's infinitesimally small creatures: and we shall begin to see God himself in his beauty. Seeing, we shall **love,** for how shall we not love God in his beauty and how shall we not love all our neighbors in whom the image of God is now visible to us? **Praise** will be the last word, for all is of God and none is of our own achievement, and we shall know the depth of gratitude and adoration. St. Augustine adds "in the end which is no end." It will be the end, for here is perfection and nothing can be more final. It will be no end, for within the resting, seeing, loving, and praising there is an inexhaustible adventure of new and ceaseless discovery. Such is the heaven for which we were created.

Resting, seeing, loving and praising: these words describe not only the goal of heaven but the message of Christianity in the world. The world has lost the way of resting, seeing, loving, praising. Swept along in ceaseless activity the world does not pause to consider. With no resting and no considering the power to see is lost: to see where we are going, to see the larger perspectives, to see beyond the group or the nation or the race, to see human beings as they really are with the image of God in them. Where seeing is dim, love becomes faint; and praise is lost for we praise only when first we have seen and loved. Man loses the praise of his creator which is the end of his existence and the source of his resting, seeing and loving.

If the words rest, see, love, and praise tell both of heaven and of the true life of man on earth, they tell no less of the Church's renewal at this and at any time. It has been all too possible in the life of the Church for rest to mean a complacently tranquil piety; for seeing to be the seeing of tradition without contemporary awareness, or the seeing of some contemporary enthusiasms without the perspective of history; for loving to be within the circle of the likeable; for praising to be a kind of aesthetic enjoyment. The renewal of the Church will mean, indeed there are signs that it does already mean, a rest which is exposed to the darkness and light of contemplation, a seeing of both the heavenly perspective and the distresses of the world, a loving which passes into costly service, and a praising which is from the depth of the soul.

While, however, renewal seems to demand the recovery of the unities of understanding which this book has tried to describe, it can never be a tidy pattern which we can know and plan. Our wisdom as well as our folly faces the darkness of Calvary and the light of Easter. Jesus suffered outside the gate, and he summons us to go out to him bearing his reproach.